WHITBREAD

250 YEARS OF BREWERY TRANSPORT

First Published in 1992 by
Roundoak Publishing,
Nynehead,
Wellington,
Somerset,
England TA21 0BX.

© **Copyright 1992**   Arthur Ingram & Roundoak Publishing

ISBN 1-871565-11-1   hardback
ISBN 1-871565-13-8   softbound

Published by Roundoak Publishing
in conjunction with Whitbread PLC

Design and typesetting by
Haight Ashbury Design,
Stoke Sub Hamdon, Somerset.

Printed in Great Britain by
The Matthews Wright Press,
Chard, Somerset.

One of the very fine photographs taken from the sets taken to show all facets of the brewery operation during the 1930s and 1940s. This view is of the South Side tanker loading bay at Chiswell Street and shows six of the 40-barrel Saurer tanks used to ferry beer in bulk to the various bottling stores of the day. None of the vehicles pictured carry headlights although they might have been removed for cleaning. The slatted 'lifesaver' guardrails which can be seen on the nearest vehicle were a safety feature of the day, aimed at preventing pedestrians falling under the rear wheels, a rather inadequate structure when compared with the designs used on vehicles today.

WHITBREAD
250 YEARS OF BREWERY TRANSPORT

ARTHUR INGRAM

Foreword by Colonel W.H. Whitbread T.D.

ROUNDOAK PUBLISHING

FOREWORD

I spent 56 years at Whitbread's, and during that time I saw the Company's transport, which has always been one of my great interests, develop from the days of the horse to modern road haulage. In between there were steam and electric, petrol lorries, the first road tanker, and then diesel.

While proud of our traditions we never hesitated to modernise where necessary our transport, the lifeblood of the business. Our immaculate vehicles and their smart drivers became a familiar sight on the roads of Britain, Belgium and in other parts of Europe, fine ambassadors for Whitbread and its products.

This book with its many fascinating photographs, tells the story of the transport revolution, both in Whitbread itself, and also in the many historic breweries who merged with us over the years.

W. H. Whitbread

Colonel W.H. Whitbread T.D.

William Henry Whitbread, who was born in 1900, joined the Company in 1924. He was appointed a managing director in 1927. In 1944, by then a Colonel, he was elected Chairman of Whitbread & Co., a post he held until 1971. Between 1948, when Whitbread's went public, and 1971, the Company's assets rose from £9 million to £241 million. From 1971 he was President of the Company before finally retiring in September 1979.

AUTHOR'S PREFACE

I like to think that it was on the strength of my previous volume 'Brewery Transport', that I was asked to prepare this review of the past 250 years of Whitbread brewery transport.

It is not often that one is asked to produce a book to celebrate a quarter-millenium, especially as this deals with one of the major companies of the British brewing industry, and I cannot hide my unashamed pride in being asked to carry out this most enjoyable of tasks.

This volume relies heavily on the memories of many people in addition to my own. Without the unstinting help of many employees and pensioners, it would not have been possible to assemble together so many interesting old photographs, and to them all, I offer my grateful thanks.

My own contribution to the story was through taking so many photographs during my years at Chiswell Street and Luton, and by relentlessly pestering anyone remotely connected with the transport fleet.

After so many years away from the Company, I have had to rely heavily upon the knowledge of Charlie Secker, Engineering Manager for the more recent happenings. He has also spent countless hours making contacts, collecting photographs, sorting slides and correcting the text. His help must be recorded and underlined.

Many of the older photographs came from the copious files kept in Whitbread Archive, and I am indebted to Nick Redman, the Company Archivist for his help and comments with this volume. Also, many thanks go to the Quadrant Picture Library/Commercial Motor for the use of their files and several period photographs which appear in this volume.

I have tried to provide a readable text covering details of the vehicles, their operation and the companies who ran them, for the present Company is successor to several hundred great family and company names which have gone to make up such a wealth of brewery history. In this respect I am indebted to H.A. Monckton for his excellent volume dealing with all the Whitbread brewery constituent companies, and this has been at my elbow during the past few months.

This slim volume seeks to trace only the transport history of Whitbread during its first 250 years. For those wishing to make a study in greater depth of the whole of the Company operations, a larger volume 'An Uncommon Brewer — The Story of Whitbread 1742-1992' by Berry Ritchie, has just been published.

In the middle 1950s the Brewery Fleet started to drift away from the dominance of the Dennis marque which had been a feature of the fleet in the immediate post-war years. A swing to the Seddon range of vehicles took place with purchases of 3-ton and 6-ton rigids for cask delivery work, plus the standard tractor models for long distance depot deliveries. In addition, one or two odd type vehicles appeared, such as a short-wheelbase tipper for the Building Department and a pair of Mark 14 rigids for trailer work, one of which is shown here. This model was classed as a 14-tonner and fitted with the Gardner 5LW engine which was rated at 94bhp. The pair of tankers and their trailers were used on the dual role of either feeding the local London bottling stores or performing journey work further afield such as Exeter, Cardiff or Leicester, for they had the advantage of being able to carry different beers in the two tanks but suffered from the disadvantage of having to have a crew of two and were somewhat slower than the rigid eight-wheelers of the day.

EARLY DAYS

When researching the early history of companies, one can sometimes be lucky and unearth photographs taken in the formative years, but with our story of Whitbread the beginnings were long before the advent of photography.

A few prints have survived the passage of time and they do give important views of the transport system in use by brewers in those far off days toward the end of the 18th century.

The first *(top right)* shows a pair of draymen carrying a cask by means of a wooden yoke or pole which distributes the weight of the cask between the two men. In the background stands a single horse four wheel dray with some large casks placed haphazardly upon it. The draymen and the cask are reasonably detailed, but the dray is only sketchy with little regard for its actual construction.

Second *(bottom right)* is an engraving by W. Ward after a painting by George Garrard, called 'A View from the East End of the Brewery, Chiswell Street', it was first published in 1792. This shows the type of dray which formed the basic design for the replica vehicle loosely termed as the Period Dray, which was built in 1950. There is plenty of life in this picture, with horses, drays, casks and draymen much in evidence.

The third picture *(far right, top)* is from the period 1825-1830 and is a reproduction of an engraving by D. Wolstenholme, taken from an aquatint produced by his father. Again there are a number of horses in this view including a pair in tandem coming into the picture from the left. The reference to drays is slight, but there are a number of people shown together with some goats, the latter being kept in the brewery for safety reasons. Evidently in the case of fire breaking out, the horses would quickly follow the goats out of the buildings to safety.

A fine view *(far right, bottom)* of the South Yard, dated 1915 by F.S. Unwin, shows two pair horse waggons, one with casks and another with sacks of malt or hop pockets. The detail shown of the buildings is very good and the inclined ramp leading to the upper storey of the stables can be seen to the left of the picture, with what appears to be a rather outsize raven on the balustrade.

WHITBREAD & HORSES

Horses and brewers have become synonymous with one another for as long as we care to remember. When Samuel Whitbread first took over his brewing business in 1742 there were 18 horses listed among the assets. Reference to old engravings of the 18th century show horses and drays much in evidence, even when casks are shown being actually carried some distance by men using wooden yokes.

The design of drays depicted in these engravings may come in for some comment, for the original artists were more concerned with the horses, and some were content to merely sketch in drays, which were after all background scenery, with little attention to detail.

One report said that there were 80 horses in use at Chiswell Street brewery in 1802, and another mentions that a visit in 1823 revealed 90 in the stables. By the 1890s pressure on the Chiswell Street site was such that new stables were erected in nearby Garrett Street, and the building housed the animals on three storeys with inclined ramps giving access to the upper floors.

The heavy old drays and waggons required large strong horses to pull them, but in 1904 a change was made in the bottling stores side of the business for lighter carts and vans which could be handled by trotting horses operating both as pairs or singles. It became the fashion for working horses to be entered into shows in the larger cities in order to improve the care shown to the animals, and reward the drivers and horsekeepers for the best kept horses in work.

So far as Whitbread was concerned the peak of the horse transport came in 1912 when there were over 400 horses in use, and with the start of the Great War in 1914

some 118 of the best were commandeered for the military.

Numbers had dropped somewhat after four years at war, but all local deliveries from Chiswell Street were still carried out by horse transport. A decision was made to gradually mechanise the delivery service, but the petrol motors were thought to pose too great a change for the men trained to look after the horses. Something of a compromise was made by introducing a small fleet of battery electric drays which had fewer controls to master, and proceeded at a pace something akin to that of a pair of horses.

From that time on the number of horses continued to fall as motor transport was deemed more efficient. So much so that by 1938 the total had shrunk to 141 and this dropped to 53 by the outbreak of WWII.

In post-war years the numbers dwindled still further, with 28 being in use in the 1950s and around 20 were held for many years after this. Although great emphasis was placed upon the horses for their publicity function in the post-war years, they continued to be used for delivery work in the inner London area. The drays and waggons were continually repaired and refurbished, and one or two show vehicles obtained from other breweries who had no further use for them.

Below: It is a pity that most horse team photographs which survive seem to portray the vehicles prepared for the local carnival or some other kind of show. This view shows specially prepared barrels on a very clean dray together with a pair of somewhat over-dressed horses ready to move off to a local event. The team is from Tennant Brothers Ltd. Sheffield which had acquired some 15 other brewery companies before passing into Whitbread control in 1961.

Left: We should be grateful that such a good photograph of a Bentley's horse-drawn dray has survived. For it not only shows the interesting style of cover at the front end, which provides a little protection for the driver as well as an anchor point for the load sheet, but also the wooden cases and wicker-covered ceramic jars that were in use in those days. At horsedrawn speeds load security was no great problem, and the sheet ties are left hanging. Note the wheel skid and chain which hang ready just ahead of the rear wheels, alongside the centre mounted ring used with the barrel rope when lowering casks into a cellar.

Right: Most of the photographs of horse-drawn vehicles discovered show them in very posed or 'set-up' circumstances, so it is good to find an occasional one which is typical of everyday operation. This photograph shows a pair just about to leave the North Side of Chiswell Street with a very neat load of kilderkins on a dray with the old style of cart wheels, in the days before they were converted to pneumatic tyres on lorry wheels. Genuine oil lamps are carried on the dray and the driver is using the issue apron, but note that he wears his own trilby, for this was in pre-war days before the bowler hats were issued to the horse draymen.

Below: A good candid photograph of a Chiswell Street pair horse dray returning to the brewery with a sizeable load of empty casks in the early 1950s. The location is probably one of the wide streets in the Islington area, and as the pair of Shires crunch their way over the newly metalled road, the photographer has managed to capture the moment when the horse driver is studying the ageing Sentinel steam tar-sprayer which stands ready to tar the next strip of road.

Below: In the past, vehicles were usually only photographed when there was some special event reckoned by the directors to be worthy of recording. This rare photograph shows three horse-drawn teams operated by the Birkenhead Brewery Co. Ltd. prepared to move off to what must have been an important event of the period. The vehicles, horses and draymen are all well turned out, and it is interesting to note that the two leading teams are arranged with the horses in tandem and not as pairs. The Birkenhead Brewery Co. dates back to 1872 and was the new name for a company formed by the amalgamation of Aspinall's Brewery and Cook's Brewery, both of Birkenhead, in 1865. Acquired by Threlfalls in 1962, the company passed to Whitbread in 1967.

Right: In researching the history of brewery transport it has been difficult to establish the first use of bulk tanks in place of wooden casks. In his book 'Seventy Rolling Years', Sir Sydney O. Nevile describes how, in 1900, he introduced what is believed to be the first road tank wagon for the transport of beer in bulk from brewery to bottling store. The success of this first vehicle, at Brandon's Putney Brewery, prompted him to patent the system of bulk delivery, and to set up The Bulk Beer Delivery Co. with a view to encouraging the use of his system for bulk deliveries to public houses. This drawing, taken from a contemporary brochure describing the system, shows a diagrammatic layout of the vehicle alongside the bulk beer storage building. The cylindrical tank is surrounded by a framework for carrying return loads of bottles mounted on a pair-horse waggon undergear. *Sydney Nevile joined the Board of Whitbreads in 1919 and soon after introduced road tankers for bulk deliveries in place of the butts and hogsheads used previously.*

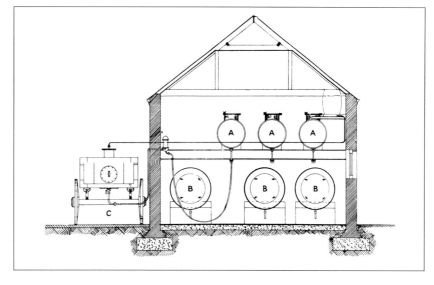

Middle right: The 1962 Whitbread Christmas Card featured a pair of Shires galloping across a field at the Hop Farm at Paddock Wood, just after being released from the company horse-box. The Daily Mirror published an article on the brewery horses and the way in which some of them were given a holiday break away from the City streets each year.

Right: When companies merge or are the subject of a takeover, there is often a feeling of loss as some of the old familiar names disappear. In 1954 when J.W. Green of Luton absorbed Flower & Sons from Stratford-upon-Avon it was assumed that the Green name would dominate, but to the surprise of many a decision was made to retain the Flowers name, and the new company took the title of Flowers Breweries Ltd. Pictured at the Northamptonshire Agricultural Show in 1956 are Lutonian Commodore and Lutonian Pippin with one of the Flowers waggons finished in the green livery which adorned the J.W. Green fleet of earlier days.

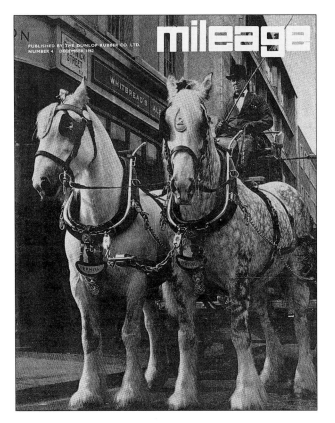

Left: Motor equipment manufacturers often report on the vehicle fleets of companies which use their products, but it is rather unusual to find one such magazine producing a story about a horse-drawn fleet. 'Mileage', the magazine of the Dunlop Rubber Co. Ltd. featured Romulus and Remus on the front cover of the December 1962 issue, which contained a story of the Whitbread Shires entitled 'Horsepower in Harness', and mentioned that some of the drays used worn Dunlop tyres which had been removed from the lorries!

Below right: Pictured outside the picturesque Garrick Inn at Stratford-upon-Avon is one of the barrel-top pair-horse waggons of the old J.W. Green company, with a pair of Whitbread greys. Several of these interesting type of waggons were disposed of during the 1950s and some remained on the forecourts of public houses. This one was rescued and refurbished at Garrett Street bodyshops and at a later date repainted from the Flowers primrose into Whitbread brown.

Below: This photograph, taken on Coronation day in 1953, shows the Speaker's Coach standing in the courtyard of the House of Commons. The horses, 'Royal' and 'Sovereign', two dapple-grey Shires from the Whitbread stables are accompanied by a driver and two walking grooms who are company draymen. The privilege of horsing this coach on great state occasions has been enjoyed by Whitbreads since 1839 when Charles Shaw Lefevre, a partner in the brewery, became Speaker of the House of Commons.

Right: Pictured outside the Park Street West, Luton brewery of J.W. Green Ltd. is this impressive display of some of the brewery horsepower. The date is sometime during WWII for the slogans on the drays and waggons refer to the 'Wings for Victory' campaign and the fact that the target of Luton town was no less than £1,425,000. The leading vehicle is an extremely low loading dray which could be likened to a barrel stillion on wheels, and it is dwarfed by the horse between the shafts. Next is a more orthodox flat waggon used mainly for bottled beer, while at the rear are two of the pair-horse, barrel-top type covered waggons which made up the major part of Green's horse-drawn fleet.

STEAMING

The steam wagon and tractor played a major part in brewery transportation in the early days of the century, for it represented the reliable alternative to the horses used previously, as well as providing greater hauling capacity for each unit.

In some instances the new means of transport was approached rather cautiously, with a small steam tractor being obtained and some of the horse vehicles being modified by fitting a metal drawbar in place of the pole or shafts used for horse draught. But this was rather a stop-gap method, for the actual carrying capacity was still limited to the size of the horse dray, and the attachment of the steam tractor produced a longer outfit than with a pair of horses, and was much less manoeuvrable.

The real alternative to horses came with the more compact steam wagon, for here was a complete vehicle which owed little to its horsed forebears, and its technical details were the result of experience with well engineered road and agricultural machinery.

The overtype of steam wagon, where the engine is placed high up in front of the driver, usually on top of a horizontal locomotive type boiler, was the basis of many early types in brewery service. Without doubt the Foden was most widely used but there were others such as Foster, Burrell, Wallis & Steevens, Tasker and Garrett to name just a few.

The other general design of wagon was known as the undertype, it having the engine located down low in the chassis frame, a layout which provided a much shorter drive between the power unit and the driven rear axle, whether that drive was by chain or shaft. Best known of the undertypes was the Sentinel, but there were others such as Yorkshire, Foden, Clayton and Garrett.

In some instances the steam wagons were only hired because the brewers thought it better to leave purchase, maintenance and staffing of the vehicles to professional haulage contractors, but the contract was often for long periods and the wagons were turned out in brewery livery.

Other brewery companies ran their own wagons, often building up considerable fleets of them. In some cases capacity was increased by the addition of trailers, as six wheelers came into fashion they adopted that design, and in a few instances there were even articulated steam wagons in service.

With the improvements of automatic stoking, pneumatic tyres and enclosed cabs the later types of steam wagon were comparable to their petrol engined rivals, and in some eyes even superior. The introduction of the diesel engine in the early 1930s, augmented by road traffic legislation of the same period, quickly depleted the steam wagon fleets up and down the country, whether they be local delivery or long distance, it did not matter. By the end of that decade it was all over, the internal combustion engine reigned supreme and the old wagon drivers were left to their memories.

Left: The change from horse traction to that of steam is well illustrated by this photograph of an early example of a 'steam motor' as they were described, towing a horse-drawn covered wagon of Wootten & Co. of Winchester. The date is probably within the first few years of this century, for Wallis & Steevens of Basingstoke, the traction engine manufacturers, were advertising their steam tractors rated at 3-tons and 4¼-tons capacity which were amply suitable for the replacement of horse traction. Wootten & Co. Ltd. was acquired by Strong & Co. of Romsey Ltd. in 1900.

Right: Taken for the vehicle builder, this photograph shows a 1900 Thornycroft steam wagon which was listed in the maker's files as a '3-ton Dray for Whitbread & Co'. The trailer is a modified horse-drawn type and both vehicle and trailer have the style of bodywork consisting of deep side raves and stout body runners onto which the casks were rolled in two rows and secured by the curved pins and chains shown at the rear. No normal flat floor was provided save for a narrow centre walkway for the loaders and vehicle crew, the casks being located by the runners toward the centre and their outer ends being carried by the side raves.

Middle right: With Bentley's Yorkshire Breweries Ltd. being located at Woodlesford some five miles south-east of Leeds, it was natural that they should look to local firms for their mechanical transport. In this photograph of the steam fleet taken within the first few years of the century, can be seen two Yorkshire undertype wagons to the left, while a Mann undertype completes the trio. The Yorkshire wagons were notable for their double-ended transverse boiler, and were built at Hunslet in south Leeds, which was close to Mann's Patent Steam Cart & Wagon Co. Ltd. works. Note that the Mann wagon unusually has dual steering fitted.

Bottom right: It is not good publicity to show vehicles which have been involved in any kind of accident, but when the subject is a slight mishap to a steam wagon some 70 years ago, then perhaps we may be forgiven for reproducing this interesting period photograph. A standard Sentinel in service with Stroud Brewery Co. Ltd. had veered off the road for some reason, luckily for the crew rescue was on hand in the shape of two Dennis vehicles, a 3½-ton Subsidy model with a crew of servicemen and a Braidwood bodied fire engine. Those with an eye for old registration numbers will note the Sentinel bears the Lanarkshire registration letter 'V' which appeared on the majority of wagons from the Polmadie works up to the time production was transferred to Shrewsbury. The lorry bears a Wiltshire registration mark of 1919, while the fire engine carries a DB mark which was allocated to Stockport C.B.C. but sometimes used by Dennis Brothers for publicity purposes.

Left: Trading under the name of the City Brewery, Norman & Pring of Exeter became a limited company in 1911, subsequently taking over two other breweries in the same city before joining Whitbreads in 1962. This photograph of their early mechanical transport shows a turn of the century Thornycroft 3/4-ton steam wagon, obviously in working condition! The Thornycroft was a popular wagon with brewers, millers and haulage contractors having won several awards in vehicle trials at the latter end of the 19th century. With a vertical water tube superheater type boiler and underfloor compound engine producing around 35hp, the chassis weighed about 3-tons.

Left: Looking back over the years when the steam wagon reigned supreme for heavyweight haulage duties, the one type which was the most popular was the Foden 5-ton overtype. The basic design had been settled upon following the maker's success in the War Office Trials of 1901, it being of a locomotive type horizontal boiler with the compound engine mounted above it and a long single chain drive to the rear axle. The example shown here was in service with W.B. Mew, Langton & Co. Ltd. and located on the Isle of Wight. The company was registered in 1887 although its origins were with the Mew family going back to the 17th century. Acquired by Strong & Co. of Romsey in 1965, the name passed into Whitbread heritage in 1968.

Left: On the 25 March 1919 the landlord of The Queen's Head at Bucks Green, West Sussex sent a picture postcard to Mr Cheeseman of the Rock Brewery at 61 St James's Street, Brighton and luckily it has survived. On the left a 5-ton Foden steam wagon waits patiently with just a wisp of steam from its chimney, while by the ancient oak, horses are being prepared for the Sussex waggon. The King & Chasemore hoarding which describes them as being 'Estate Agents and Timber Surveyors', is covered with notices of property sale including The Green Dragon at Horsham just 6¾ miles away by the signpost.

Below right: Early Whitbread records show that the steam vehicles were owned by transport contractors although painted in the company livery, a system much used by brewers of the period where only the local delivery fleet was actually company owned. This rather grainy photograph shows a Leyland steam wagon in carnival dress complete with First Prize cup and an obviously happy driver! It could possibly have been owned by H. Viney of Preston who ran a fleet of Leyland steam wagons and could well have distributed beer to the local depots from supplies sent by rail or sea to Preston or Liverpool.

Below: There were many steam wagons in brewery service, but the articulated type shown here was by no means so widespread in use, many operators preferring the use of a drawbar trailer with their wagons in order to achieve greater payload. This Portsmouth United Breweries Foden wagon dates from the mid-1920s, and is pictured decorated for some unidentified event later in its life. The heads of the casks are marked 'PUB IPA MALTA', indicating that the load was destined for the Mediterranean island, but whether it was an export order or a load destined for one of HM Ships, is not clear. Portsmouth United Breweries was established at Elm Street, Southsea, but this vehicle carries the King Street address following the acquisition of Rock Brewery (Brighton) Ltd. in 1927.

Right: Unfortunately this photograph of the Brickwoods fleet in the late 1920s has suffered through the passage of time, having been folded for storage. Never-the-less it does show some eight Foden steam wagons together with a couple of Thornycroft petrol lorries in the far distance. Interestingly the second wagon is lettered for S. & T.N. Blake & Co. Ltd. of South Cross Street Brewery in Gosport, a company which was acquired by Brickwoods in 1926.

Below: Pictured whilst delivering to the Taswell Arms in Southsea, this recently-delivered 1928 Foden six-wheeler was rated as a 10/12-ton payload machine, and was naturally a development of this makers very popular overtype wagon. This style of bodywork was not common among brewers of the period for it represents a van with slatted sides; perhaps the brewers were anxious not to have the rain wash off the bottle labels, or the summer sun spoil their cask beers. With the wagon parked halfway across the street it does look as though the picture has been arranged, but the draymen and the casks appear to be everyday and in no way specially set-up for the photograph.

Middle right: It is generally acknowledged that the ultimate in steam wagon design was reached during the 1930s by the Sentinel. With its underfloor engine, shaft drive and pneumatic tyre equipment the vehicles were well able to hold their own against the internal combustion contemporaries, although they suffered from the legislators because of their marginally higher unladen weight. This 1934 example was one of a handful which handled some of the Fremlins deliveries in Kent and was turned out in their mid brown livery complete with the famous Elephant trade mark and the 'Kent's Best' slogan which had been used earlier by George Beer & Rigden. With the topicality of the ozone layer, one wonders if the soft drink brand name in the background is worthy of resurrection!

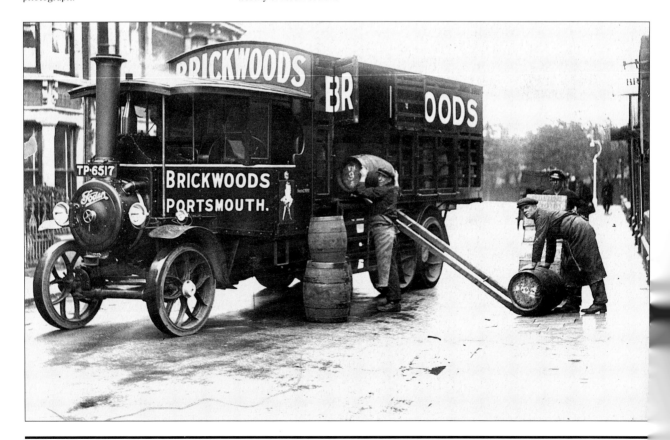

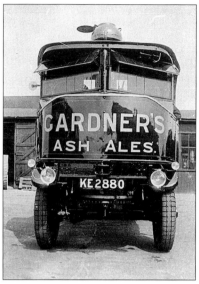

Above: Gardner & Co. of Ash in Kent, was established in 1898 and after absorbing two other small breweries in the second and third decades, was itself taken over by Tomson & Wotton Ltd. in 1951 to form Combined Breweries (Holding) Ltd. It is not certain whether this 1921 Sentinel steam waggon was originally owned by the company, but this photograph shows it in their livery after undergoing an overhaul which included the fitting of pneumatic tyres and the provision of all electric lighting. An electric klaxon horn is fitted under the roof canopy and a spark arrestor has been added to the exhaust chimney, a useful adjunct when working in agricultural areas, so as not to be liable for any crop fires.

Left: Pictured soon after the amalgamation of George Beer of Canterbury and W.E. & J. Rigden of Faversham which took place in 1922, this Clayton 6-ton steam wagon was one of four in service with the new company of George Beer & Rigden. They were owned by the Wingham Engineering Co. Ltd. who supplied them on long term contract to the brewers, suitably liveried and complete with driver. Later in life the wagons were converted to pneumatic tyres.

ESTD 1742

DRIVE ELECTRIC

A s mentioned elsewhere, Whitbread director Sydney O. (later Sir Sydney) Nevile seems to have exerted a considerable influence over brewery transport policy, firstly with his patented Bulk Beer Delivery System connected to which was his desire to see beer moved in bulk rather than in the comparatively small wooden casks.

Soon after his arrival at Whitbreads in 1919 he was urging his fellow directors to consider the use of more motor vehicles for beer delivery, noticing the rapid expansion of the motors following the Great War. Although heavy steam motors had been in use for some time, some of the heavy type of petrol motors were rather prone to breakdown and required frequent adjustment and repair. They also

Below: The first six of the electric fleet lined up in the North Yard of Chiswell Street, with the Middle Stage on the left and the sundial over to the right. It is difficult to decide which colour the vehicles are painted, but with each trio being a different shade it suggests that the first three are painted in brown with the remaining three finished in the old green colour. Although no fleet numbers are shown, they are in fact numbers 4, 5, 6, 2, 1 and 3 reading from left to right. On the original photograph it is possible to read the Emergency Vehicle Numbers which show E for electric and City 2 as the Whitbread fleet code.

required some degree of skill in handling, with their narrow solid tyres, heavy steering, two wheel brakes and rather recalcitrant power units.

Relying on his experience at Brandon's Brewery at Putney where some electric vehicles were used for local deliveries, he urged Whitbreads to do the same, arguing that the electric was much easier to handle than its petrol-powered counterpart and therefore it would be easier to retrain men used to driving horse vehicles.

So in 1920 an order was placed with the General Vehicle Co. for a batch of 3½-ton battery electric lorries which were to be employed on delivery work in the inner London area. It was envisaged that they would work within a ten mile radius of Chiswell Street, well within the capabilities of the expected 30-mile journey possible with a fully-charged battery.

When the 1921 Commercial Motor Exhibition opened at Olympia on 14th October, one of the Whitbread GV electrics was displayed on Stand 66 of the General Vehicle Co., and a contemporary report says that it was part of 'a large fleet' and carried an authentic load of barrels.

In all, 15 of the electric lorries were used in the Chiswell Street fleet, which was made up of 13 3½-ton and two 5-ton models. The 3½-ton model had a wheelbase of 11ft 0½in and the Exide Ironclad battery of 44 cells was rated at 252 ampere-hours and weighed well over a ton. A speed of 8-10 mph was recommended.

The general layout of the vehicles was with the batteries mounted in two boxes which were positioned in the centre of the vehicle on the outside of the parallel chassis frame. A five position controller fed the current to a single, series-wound electric motor positioned just ahead of the rear axle. The drive was made via a single roller chain in an oil bath to the countershaft mounted in front of the motor, and thence by two outer sprockets which contained the handbrake mechanism, two long open roller chains connected to large sprockets on the rear wheels.

The 5-ton version of the GV electric was generally similar to that of the 3½-ton model, differing in such details as longer wheelbase and overall length, and was slightly wider and carried a larger battery which weighed an extra 300 lbs.

During the 1930s the electrics were updated by converting the axles to take steel disc type lorry wheels so that pneumatic tyres could be fitted, and some of the fleet had refurbished cabs incorporating proper windscreens.

Although the electric vehicle is much simpler than its petrol driven rival, and has far fewer moving parts, they were not without their problems. The open drive chains suffered from wear and stretching and of course there were plenty of occasions when the fitters had to tow in vehicles because of flat batteries.

The electric vehicle was quite popular during the 1920s and 1930s for a wide variety of delivery tasks and several other brewers took them into their fleets. The Whitbread electrics were phased out in the post-war period when the reasons for their existence no longer applied. Some were scrapped but several saw further service in the hands of other London brewers for a few years longer.

Below: Pictured in Whitecross Street just outside the Silk Street garage, No. 5 electric is shown after its last repaint before being sold out of service. The date is probably about 1946 for it was in the early post-war years when the renumbering of the brewery fleet took place when prefix letters were added to the vehicle numbers. The reasoning behind this move was to make the numbers more readily recognisable by all those connected with the fleet. This vehicle was one of the few which received a proper windscreen during one of the refurbishments which took place during the vehicles long life-time.

Left: A scene inside the Silk Street maintenance garage of Chiswell Street brewery in 1947 with electric No. 6 undergoing one of the regular services. Whilst the foreman checks the inside of the cab a fitter uses a hand pump to grease the brake gear. Note that the off-side body gate has been removed and taken to the body-shop for repair.

Below: This photograph shows the first of the GV electric vehicles leaving the North Side of the Chiswell Street site sometime in 1920. It might possibly be a demonstrator for the manufacturer, for the lettering appears to have been added to the photograph, and was perhaps on trial before a firm order was placed. There is much activity in the Middle Stage area behind, with a couple of Foden steam wagons and horse drays being loaded, whilst a very high load of hops is being hauled into the hop store on the second floor.

Right: Electric No. 4 in what could be described as the interim stage of their life — refurbished with pneumatic tyres, but still retaining the open cab. In this rather grainy photograph the barrel skid can just be seen inside the body, and the positioning of the lights and the klaxon horn show the variety of changes which took place over the years.

Below right: Nearside view of one of the electrics in the North Yard of Chiswell Street showing it with pneumatic tyres but still retaining the open-fronted cab. The large electric motor can just be made out positioned just ahead of the rear axle, and the large battery boxes are very evident slung beneath the body. This photograph shows the lettering layout in use before the introduction of the hinds head emblem on the cab and body sides.

Below: Genuine street scenes showing company vehicles are rare, and this photograph of electric No. 14 is all the more interesting because it is one of the large series issued by Judges' Postcards. Dated circa 1926 it is entitled 'The Arm of the Law' and shows the point-duty police constable wearing his light coloured cape. Contemporary London traffic of a horsed cart and box delivery tricycle complete the nostalgic scene.

PETROL PROPULSION

S ome of the brewers took to using the new petrol engined vehicles quite early in the century, while others tended to keep them at arms length for a few years, preferring the horses which had served them so well.

So far as early records show, the first Whitbread petrol motor was obtained in 1909, it being a product of Dennis Brothers of Guildford in Surrey, a company which began producing motorised vehicles well before the turn of the century. The company gained many customers because of their worm and wheel final drive, which was much quieter than many of its competitors who used bevel gears, or even stuck to the noisy chain drives.

Whitbread's affair with Dennis was to be sustained for many years, right through to the 1960s in fact, with the Pax V and the Maxim playing the finale.

It is not as though the Dennis was used to the exclusion of all else, for the early fleet list does prove that alternatives were tried at various times, these including Tilling Stevens, Thornycroft, Ford, Belsize, Leyland, Vulcan, Albion, Maxwell, Halley and Bean, although none in great numbers.

One report on the very early trials with motors mentions the fact that "valuable advice was given by Mr. E.A. Turner during the days when we first tried petrol motors, and later during the war period." This original contact was to grow firmer and be maintained for the next half-century, for the said gentleman and his company was to be instrumental in the design of Whitbread vehicles in collaboration with the various transport managers during that period. This was the reason why the majority of vehicles bore Surrey registration marks, for the E.A. Turner body works was established at Kingston in Surrey.

Below: It is provident that the photographer of this, reputedly the first petrol motor lorry bought by the company, included the two draymen, for it enables us to have an authentic and everyday view of a period crew. Although the nice white load sheet is lettered as Kingston depot, the cab side carries the Chiswell Street address. This 1909 Dennis was the precursor of many vehicles from the Guildford manufacturer to carry the Whitbread name over the next 50 years. It is worth noting that no headlamp is carried on the vehicle although a stirrup fixing is provided, and the oil sidelights were probably thought adequate for normal daily delivery work. A tiny hind-head trademark adorns the radiator header tank and the filler cap carries the badge of the Commercial Motor Users Association — forerunner of today's Freight Transport Association.

At this juncture it might be beneficial to explain one curious point about the Whitbread transport fleet, or fleets to be precise. Ever since the partnerships which existed in the century before the establishment of Whitbread & Company Limited in 1889, bottled beer production had been looked upon almost as a separate organisation, with its headquarters being established at Grays Inn Road near Kings Cross in 1870, and Britannia Street coming into use in 1889.

The Brewery at Chiswell Street is reported as using its first mechanical vehicle in 1903 — a steam wagon — but this was supplied by a contractor. Another record shows that a Thornycroft was in use in 1900, this time towing a converted horse cart. The brewery seems to have held on to its horses for local deliveries for a long while, using contractors and the railways for longer distances, plus of course coastal shipping for those depots which could be reached easily by water.

So we have a situation where two parts of the same company were beginning to introduce mechanical transport, quite independent of one another. The Brewery fleet was concerned with making deliveries of cask beer to the houses in the London area, supplying cask beer to the growing number of provincial depots and gradually increasing the supply of beer in large butts and hogsheads for the rapidly expanding bottled beer trade. Some of these movements could be handled by horses, some required heavier vehicles, while other traffic was handled by rail and sea.

The Bottling Stores also had varying demands on its distribution system, for it was required to supply local houses and other outlets, the widespread network of depots being opened around the country, and the onward transport to the customers supplied by those depots. From 1904 it also had the problem of supplying an increasing market in continental Europe as first Brussels, and later Antwerp depots were opened.

When studying old photographs the early vehicles appear to have been numbered according to each depot, and it is not certain when the first general numbering system for the whole of the two fleets came about. The Brewery fleet seems to have undergone several renumberings during its sixty or so years existence, and the electrics were numbered in a series all of their own. Plain numbers were used up until about 1946 when a new system was devised which added prefix letter codes to denote the vehicle make, with the electrics understandably being coded 'E'. The majority of this fleet carried London registration marks.

The Bottling Stores fleet carried plain numbers throughout their separate existence up to number 969 after which they received prefix codes, the Brewery fleet finishing up with S177 before it was amalgamated into a common fleet numbering system.

Above: Established by Thomas Wethered in 1788, the Marlow based brewery remained in family hands up to 1899 when it became a limited company, and was acquired by Strong & Co. of Romsey in 1949 and joined the Whitbread group in 1968. The company transport was probably unique in the industry by way of its perpetuation of names for all its vehicles, which are said to have originated with the horses employed in the early days of the company, the original nameplates being transferred as vehicles are replaced. It would appear that vehicle crew, customers and landlady have all savoured the moment when the photographer was able to record 'Always' making a delivery to The Wheatsheaf. The vehicle is a rare petrol engined product of the Aveling & Porter works at Rochester in Kent who were better known as builders of steam vehicles particularly road-rollers, and the prancing horse emblem graced many smokebox doors of council steam rollers up to the 1950s.

Below: Many of the photographs used in this book were sent in by retired employees, and some have suffered the wear of time, but they never-the-less lose none of the atmosphere of days gone by. Typical is this view of a chain-driven Albion of pre Great War days pictured whilst making a delivery to a hotel customer of Rhondda Valley Breweries Ltd. Although the drayman has the customary leather apron for handling the casks, the driver sports a long jacket and leather gaiters, the latter no doubt as protection against the cold draught which came up through the floorboards around the foot pedals. Note that the vehicle has an open chain drive which was handy for adjustment as the chains stretched with use, but they left the drive wide open for the ingress of road grit and dirt which caused rapid wear to the links. The posing whippet is probably owned by the hotel-keeper and is not a vehicle mascot!

Left: The Worksop & Retford Brewery Co. was registered in 1881 being created from the Priorwell Brewery Co. and Smith & Nephew of Cresswell Holme Brewery, both in the town of Worksop at the northern end of Sherwood Forest. This early motor lorry of about 1906 is pictured carefully posed with the cask heads all the right way up, and the crew justifiably proud of their new vehicle, which is a rather rare 4-ton model produced by Sir W.G. Armstrong, Whitworth & Co. of Newcastle-upon-Tyne.

Below: Pictured beneath the famous sundial which remains aloft in the old north yard of Chiswell Street, and to this day gives its name to the present court, one of the 1920s Thornycroft cask delivery fleet stands empty, at a time when the fleet was being modernised. The simple lines of the vehicle present a clear view of the straight chassis side rails which taper slightly to the rear just beyond the rearmost spring hanger brackets, and the longitudinal body runners with their six transverse cross bearers can be easily seen. Inside the body the load sheet stands in a roll at the front, with the strong barrel rope loosely coiled on the floor and the barrel skid lays upside-down pointing toward the hinged tailboard. The lettering on the body sides could hardly be larger, but there is no sign of any trademark or hinds head, the management of the day probably reasoning that the name was advertisement enough. The well-washed yard surface serves to highlight the very small contact area afforded by the narrow solid tyres of the day.

Right: Current day distribution managers will wince at the idea of a four-man crew being used for a 3-ton delivery vehicle! This Rhymney Breweries lorry, posed outside the brewery gate with its A N D R E W B U C H A N clock-face, has probably gained a couple of brewery workers for the photograph. The vehicle is one of a number of J-type Thornycroft subsidy chassis used by the company, the Great War model which gained much admiration from our soldiers in France during that conflict. Old vehicle enthusiasts will probably note the legend 'P.New.813' painted on the dash panel, this being a vehicle registration system created in the post-war period in order to record all vehicles available in times of emergency. The 'P' stands for petrol vehicle, and the 'New' for the local registration town of Newport which was in Monmouthshire in those days.

Right: In the early days of motor vehicle development, long before the advent of nation-wide distributorships, it was natural for brewers, like many other industrialists, to purchase their transport locally. Being located in Maidstone, Kent the four Fremlin brothers acquired a number of Tilling vehicles from the nearby works of Tilling-Stevens Ltd. This particular model was unusual in the fact that it was a gear driven vehicle, that is with an engine, clutch and gearbox much like the vehicles of today. For the firm of Tilling-Stevens was far better known for its petrol-electric chassis, where the petrol engine drove an electric generator which in turn supplied power to electric motors which performed the final drive to the road wheels.

Right: Tomson & Wotton was trading in the Ramsgate area for many years prior to becoming registered as a Limited company in 1892. In 1951 they joined with Gardner & Co. Ltd. of Ash to form Combined Breweries (Holdings) Ltd. and this company was absorbed by Whitbread in 1968. For many years Tomson & Wotton used a grinning man's face as a kind of trade mark, and an example is shown on the headboard of this S&D Freighter. Whether this little truck was owned by the brewery when it was used in a carnival procession at the seaside town of Ramsgate is not certain, but the type was certainly not common among brewery fleets, it being more at home serving as the basis for refuse vehicles for local councils.

Left: Although Jude, Hanbury & Co. Ltd. were established in Wateringbury, Kent a move was made to Canterbury following the acquisition of Ash's East Kent Brewery Co. Ltd. in 1924. This photograph shows a line-up of the delivery fleet soon after this date, for the vehicles show the Canterbury address. The Leyland on the left of the picture was the latest addition, it being carried on the new pneumatic tyres in contrast to the remainder of the fleet which are on solids. The second Leyland was also of quite recent registration and carries an illuminated sign on the cab roof. Next to it is one of the locally built Tilling-Stevens petrol-electric vehicles of the early 1920s while the three remaining vehicles are Sentinel steam waggons from earlier days. The garage is worthy of note, for it has separate doors to each vehicle bay and individual roof vents to expel the smoke and exhaust fumes.

Middle right: Many brewers tried to increase their total sales by encouraging the habit of drinking in the home, and in fact many people who enjoyed a glass of beer never ventured into a public house. The 'take-home' trade as it was sometimes called placed great emphasis on the local off-licence and those with an eye for expansion went to great lengths to expand their sales area through a home delivery service. In areas of high density housing the delivery cycle was adequate for supplies close to the shop, but for outlying areas a small van was a distinct advantage. Mr. Plume had a thriving business in Station Road, Chadwell Heath and in the 1920s was enjoying an expanding trade as many people moved out of the squalid areas close to the city to enjoy the more spaceful surroundings of the near-Essex countryside. His model T Ford was well turned out and quite capable of carrying many deliveries, being rated at all of 10-cwt capacity within the tasteful boarded tilt body.

Bottom right: This page from a sales brochure of the period shows one of the fleet of Commercar vehicles used by J.W. Green of Luton, Beds. in the period following the 1914-1918 war. The company always favoured covered vehicles rather than the plain open lorries employed by most brewers of the day, a design which went back to their horse-drawn wagons, one of which survived to see the Whitbread takeover in 1962. Commercars were established in 1905 and moved to Luton in 1907, gaining much publicity from their use of the Linley pre-selector type gearbox which had a distinct advantage over the straight-tooth 'crash' type gearboxes which graced most of the competitive vehicles. Note that this example sports electric lighting as opposed to the oil and acetylene lamps with which most other vehicles were fitted.

Left: Straight out of the paintshop, this large articulated Scammell with dropframe carrier, or semi-trailer in today's terms, poses in Tolpits Lane near the Watford factory of its builders. This particular vehicle represented the latest design for the bulk transport of goods, and although having a legal maximum speed of just 12 mph was a decided improvement on the heavy steam vehicles of the day. The Scammell was the largest motor vehicle of the period, and the first heavy articulated lorry to be produced in large numbers, its design being said to emanate from the Great War experience of Colonel Scammell with the American Knox, a design of tractor used by heavy haulage contractors in the 1920s.

Below: Posed in the road outside the Basingstoke works this dainty Thornycroft dates from before the Great War, and is a splendid example of the quality produced by the mid-Hampshire vehicle builder. With its coach-built cab embodying tongue-and-groove panelling and a fine livery heightened by elaborate lining which even extends to the body crossbearers, it was typical of traditional brewery quality. The vehicle was probably based at the Tiverton brewery of the erstwhile Thomas Ford & Son which although taken over in 1895 by Starkey, Knight & Co. still retained such local demand that the headboard is lettered as Ford's Tiverton Beer.

A " Commer Car " in the Brewing Trade.

PROGRESS & EXPANSION

O nce the design of the motor lorry had settled down to an established layout, using modern materials and backed up with regular servicing and proven reliability, its use spread throughout the industry.

So far as Whitbread was concerned the transport fleet was built up around a core of vehicles in the 4-ton payload capacity type, which had a unladen weight of around 2½-tons. There were others of lighter and heavier type but these made up a small part of the total.

The bulk of the fleet for many years was a four wheel vehicle for local deliveries, with the larger six- and eight-wheel types being reserved for the long distance work. But even in the 1930s there were a number of articulated vehicles in use, although they were in the fleets of contractors.

The Bottling Stores fleet at this time was about 160 vehicles strong, with Dennis, Leyland, AEC, Albion, Commer and Morris makes, covering payloads from 8cwt through to 15-tons. Of this fleet, 30 were commandeered for military use at the outbreak of WWII and a further two were acquired by the Ministry of War Transport for official duties.

The Brewery Fleet was much smaller, with a total of around 30 in the year before WWII, these being mainly of Albion and Saurer manufacture.

In the early post-war years the Brewery fleet had increased to 52 with the major player still being Saurer, but with Dennis moving up fast. Over in the Bottling Stores the 1947 fleet strength was 180 with Dennis being the major supplier with 128, while Bedford, Leyland and Dodge could just make 32 between them. But still the diesel engine was kept at bay by the brewers, for it was said that they thought the diesel fumes would be injurious to their beer.

Gradually the transport fleet expanded in line with increased trade and the number of houses and accounts on the books. The gradual swing to palletised loading in the 1960s, plus the move toward articulation provided a stimulus for new types to be tried. The stalwart Dennis's were supplanted by AEC, Seddon and Atkinson units, and then these in turn were replaced by new names in the fleet such

as Scammell, ERF, Foden, Volvo, Ford and latterly by Mercedes-Benz.

Road tanker capacities have always had to be kept in line with the size of storage vessels at breweries and production plants, and the growth in this area has been phenomenal. In the 1920s it was usual for tanks to be of 20 to 30 barrel capacity, this increasing in the 1930s to perhaps 40-barrels. In the post-war era a large number of 80-barrel tankers were added to the fleet and later these were joined by the 120-barrel tanks as road transport regulations were relaxed to allow 32-ton gross weights. More recently still we have seen the maximum gross weight regulations move to 38-tonnes which now allows a tank capacity of 155-barrels.

The large vehicle used in the Primary Fleet is

moving toward a standard of a two-axle tractor with a tri-axle semi-trailer with bodywork being of either tank or curtain-sided type. The tankers have a capacity of 155-barrels which is not variable, but the other trailers used for bottle, can or container beer can achieve a loading of 26-tonnes in complete safety, a low centre of gravity concept being adopted with a fifth-wheel height of 51".

To this end, a series of Stability Tests were carried out at the Motor Industry Research Association proving ground at Nuneaton. The first tested was a Volvo F7 tractor with a Crane Fruehauf semi-trailer grossing at 32-tons, then in May 1983 came the first in a series of tests with 38-tonne gross weight combinations using Volvo F12, Ford, ERF, Foden and Mercedes-Benz tractors with CF tri-axle trailers.

The tests were conducted on a continuous circular track. The speed of the combination was gradually increased until a 5% roll was possible with a 'g' force of .31 being recorded. As a result of these prolonged tests an industry standard has been established which sets down a force of .35g being obtained without roll-over.

Naturally the load inside the trailer is itself subjected to a considerable force as the vehicle is progressively pushed round the circuit, and the side curtains are assisted by internal load restraints attached to the floor and the roof of the trailer.

The 1990s sees the Primary Fleet standardising on a range of lightweight tractors including the Foden 4000 series powered by a Cummins engine and the Mercedes-Benz 1733 model which incorporates that maker's own 330bhp power unit. The semi-trailers will be air sprung tri-axle types by Crane Fruehauf which are scheduled to have a ten year life. In the light of operating experience this could well be extended to 15 years unless legislation restrictions intervene earlier.

Thomas Wethered & Sons Ltd. of Marlow were staunch supporters of Thornycroft lorries during the time that the marque was in production, and their J-type 'Perseverance' has luckily remained with the company since it was built in 1919. They were also very proud of the awards gained at the various Brewers Exhibitions, so much so that this 1929 model has a selection of the medallions displayed on the cab side. Wethereds also stayed with the same style of body for very many years: notice that the sides are quite low. Careful study reveals that the body standards are set in from the side of the floor, and that six 'shorestaffs' are provided on the outside to help withstand the buffeting of heavy casks. The paint scheme is worthy of note: even the body runners and crossbearers are tastefully chamfered and lined out. A new type of roof sign has been specified for this vehicle, a vertical mirror reflecting the name image which utilises natural daylight for the illumination.

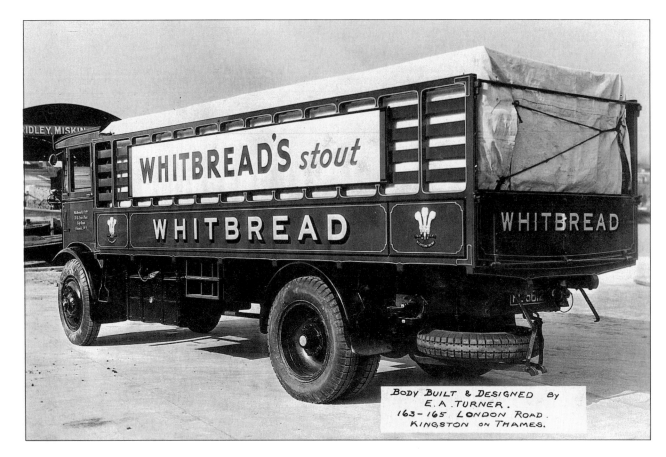

BODY BUILT & DESIGNED BY
E. A. TURNER.
163-165 LONDON ROAD.
KINGSTON ON THAMES.

Left: This 1931 photograph shows one of the largest vehicles employed at that time, it being a 6-ton Dennis and shows clearly the method of fitting the tailored sheet over the load and totally within the body. As the label explains, the bodywork was carried out by E.A. Turner of Kingston, who were the main supplier of Dennis vehicles to the company for many years as well as being a regular bodybuilder for the fleet. The very high sides of the body are fixed in order to secure the load and access is only possible from the rear where a hinged tailboard and single metal bar secure the load, the sheet merely being to protect the beer from the sun and rain. This type of vehicle was for long distance trunk work between bottling stores and distribution depots, so no side access was required for house deliveries.

Top right: Even a steady drizzle fails to dull the polished aluminium bonnet of this fine Thornycroft as it is posed for its pre-delivery photograph in the works yard at Basingstoke in 1930. The body is carried up to the cab roof height in order to retain the mixed loads which were the order of the day, and which on a long run could mean much sorting of empties en route. The Stroud Brewery Co. had gained Limited Company status in 1888, and by 1958 the company had acquired a dozen smaller brewers and then joined the Cheltenham & Hereford Breweries Ltd. to form West Country Brewery Holdings Ltd., finally coming under the Whitbread title in 1963.

Middle right: Taken from an Albion Motors brochure of the period, this illustration shows one of the early 1930s fleet during the days when the greater part of deliveries consisted of cask beer, with the larger houses taking their stock in 36-gallon casks. As a sign of the times the caption to the original photograph is worth quoting in full — "The Cheltenham Original Brewery Co. Ltd. use two 35/55HP Albion 4-tonners for deliveries. An attractive feature of this model is its low floor level of 3' 7½" which makes for very easy loading where no platform is available." One wonders what the draymen would have to say about that!

Bottom right: Jonas Alexander & Sons Ltd. was a company registered in 1927 to carry on the business of J. Alexander and J.M. Hesford at Kendal in Westmorland. They were succeeded by Dutton's Blackburn Brewery in 1947 who in turn joined Whitbread in 1964. This Thornycroft dates from the early 1930s and is a small machine of about 30-cwt to 2-tons payload. It was probably called upon to carry a mixed load from the Beezon Brewery which included wines and spirits, and a platform body with a sheet and ropes was considered adequate.

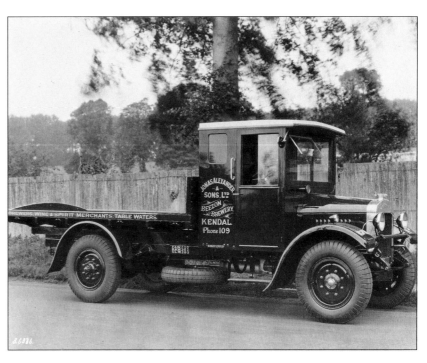

Left: During 1933 The Cheltenham Original Brewery Co. took delivery of three Albion 40/45-cwt lorries, one of which is shown here. With much of the trade of the time being in large size casks, the use of a flat platform body was considered adequate. With the loaded casks weighing 3 to 4-cwt each, the ten or so which went to make up the load could be roped at the rear, and the friction between cask and wooden floor relied upon to keep the load from slipping.

Above: One of the successful chassis models produced by Dennis Brothers during the 1930s was the 'Lancet' which was available modified for either lorry or bus work. This 1934 example for Fremlins shows the normal-control or bonneted version of the chassis, complete with platform body which has a hinged tailboard. Just visible are the deep body cross members which were necessary to bring the floor up to the height of the loading bank, for this was basically a bus chassis designed for a low bodywork.

Right: Dennis Brothers of Guildford were justly proud of their close relationship with Whitbreads over very many years, and the number of vehicles that they had supplied to the company was mentioned in their publicity material. The 1928 edition of the Dennis sales brochure featured a Whitbread vehicle on the front cover and carried the caption "This 6-ton Lorry is one of Messrs. Whitbread's fleet of more than 130 Dennis vehicles". This generation of vehicles featured a Dennis engine of 110 x 150 mm bore and stroke which was rated as 50hp/70bhp driving by means of a cone clutch and four speed straight tooth gearbox to an overhead worm drive rear axle. Interesting to note that electric headlamps were supplied but sidelights were still oil. This was because ignition was by high tension magneto and engine starting facilitated by hand cranking—no battery or electric starter being fitted. To provide electric lighting while the vehicle was at rest would mean keeping the engine running, a condition not to be tolerated with a vehicle standing for long periods.

Bottom right: Destined for the bottling store at Ceres Road, Kingston-upon-Thames, this 2-tonner was one of 22 Dennis machines delivered during 1930. In the same year a Ford model A was acquired for the Belgian operation and a solitary Leyland TQ1 'Buffalo' bought for comparison with the Dennis 6-tonners included in the fleet. The crew of the model illustrated have the advantage of an opening windscreen, roll-down side curtains and electric lighting, but a peep inside the cab would have revealed a fixed bench seat and just a narrow padded backrest between their spine and the back framing of the cab! Note that the radiator mascot is the Whitbread man in the shape of a bottle, and not the usual hinds head.

Left: Pictured in a corner of the cask yard at the Trueman Street, Liverpool brewery of Threlfalls Brewery Co. Ltd., are this pair of AEC vehicles. The date is probably 1936, for this was when the company took delivery of some new 'Matador' chassis from the Southall works, and took the opportunity to show the new model alongside a model from ten years earlier. Although both vehicles are equipped with pneumatic tyres and electric lighting, the progression with cab design is most noticeable, though the new vehicle still retains a fixed starting handle.

BY APPOINTMENT TO
H.M. THE KING

This 6-Ton Lorry is one of Messrs. Whitbread's fleet of more than 130 Dennis vehicles.

COMMERCIAL VEHICLES

| 2½-TONS | 3-TONS |
| 4-TONS | 6-TONS |

(For 30 cwt. Chassis, see separate catalogue)

Telephones: Guildford 1575 (6 lines)
Telegrams: "Dennis, Guildford."
Codes: A.B.C. (5th Edition), Lieber's, Bentley's and Marconi

DENNIS BROS. LTD.
Motor Lorry Manufacturers to H.M. The King
GUILDFORD
ENGLAND

Left: Most brewers who used open vehicle for their cask and bottled beer deliverie realised that a covered vehicle was imperativ for the handling of wines, spirits, mineral etc. Much of this type of commodity was fc off-licences and needed to be protected fron the weather and from pilferage. Thi photograph shows a WH model Bedfor turned out in the two-tone green and whit livery of Green's during the 1930s. Note th soda syphon type radiator ornament — nc working presumably.

Below: This 1938 photograph shows a batch o eleven WTL model Bedfords, all wit consecutive registration numbers, lined up o the cobbles outside the Market Hall of th home town of Dutton's Blackburn Brewer Co. Ltd. The origin of Duttons goes back t 1799 when Thomas Dutton and his son Williar

Right: Spreckley Brothers Ltd. was registered in 1897 to take over the business of Worcester brewers Spreckley Brothers and George Joseland & Sons. In 1958 the company was acquired by Cheltenham & Hereford Breweries Ltd. which in turn passed to Whitbread via West Country Brewery Holdings Ltd. in 1963. This example of the Spreckley fleet is a rather diminutive Thornycroft A2 model of the early 1930s — probably rated to carry about 30-cwt. The flat platform body and large fixed tailboard suggest that it was employed mostly on bottled beer or wine and spirit deliveries.

set up the business at the Salford Brewery in Bow Street, Blackburn. It is interesting to note that ten of this batch of Bedfords had the stanchion and chain type of bodywork, while the eleventh, on the extreme right of the picture, has slatted bodywork indicating that it was probably used for a variety of work.

Left: One of the additions to the fleet of Strong & Co. during 19.. was this Thornycroft with an unusual type of high-sided body with dr.. sides for half its length. It is a 4-ton 'Sturdy' model PC with the make. HB4 engine which was rated at 30.6hp. The 14'-0" wheelbase chass.. mounted on 34x7 tyres sold for just £770!

Top right: Pictured in the yard at Wateringbury, this AEC 'Mammo.. Major' is the Mark II model and was supplied to Frederick Leney and So.. Ltd. in 1939. The style of bodywork is unusual, for it appears to be t.. Whitbread style of fixed sides but with a very high framework added. T.. use of a sheet all round the inside of the body and over the load promp.. the question as to whether its use was to carry pockets of hops, or is .. that protection for everyday loads of bottled beer?

Left: Long & Co. (Southsea) Ltd. was register.. in 1924 and acquired by Brickwoods Ltd. .. 1933. About 1930 they took delivery of th.. neat little A2 model Thornycroft whic.. judging by the dropside body fitted, w.. destined for wine and spirit deliveries rath.. than being employed on heavy cask work. T.. fact that the company had received the Roy.. Warrant was publicised by the signboa.. mounted high up on the cab roof, where.. could be sure of being noticed. The tyres ha.. been specially painted for this wor.. photograph which shows the livery and lini.. to advantage, but unfortunately the noond.. sun has bleached out the cabside paintings.. awards gained for their quality ale.

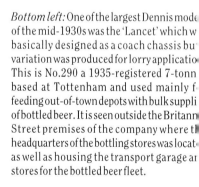

Bottom left: One of the largest Dennis mode.. of the mid-1930s was the 'Lancet' which w.. basically designed as a coach chassis bu.. variation was produced for lorry applicatio.. This is No.290 a 1935-registered 7-tonn.. based at Tottenham and used mainly f.. feeding out-of-town depots with bulk suppli.. of bottled beer. It is seen outside the Britann.. Street premises of the company where t.. headquarters of the bottling stores was locat.. as well as housing the transport garage a.. stores for the bottled beer fleet.

Right: In 1937 the company started to acqui.. vehicles of its own in the maximum capaci.. class, rather than rely upon those suppli.. under contract by General Roadways, an.. pair of AEC 'Mammoth Major' rigid eig.. wheelers were employed on trunk work fro.. the London bottling stores to the larg.. provincial depots. In this AEC photograph t.. second machine of the pair is pictured leavi.. Chiswick bottling stores and the gateman.. shown dutifully checking out the load. The o.. iron gateway with its illuminated gold-colo.. name is a nice period touch, as is the noti.. offering employment to a wide choice .. persons in those days of full employment!

Above: Describing themselves as 'Automobile, Aero, Maritime and Radio Engineers', Surtees of Bevan Street, Lowestoft were responsible for supplying these four 4-ton Dodge Brothers vehicles to Lacons of Great Yarmouth in December 1936. Unlike many other brewers, Lacons favoured the use of flat platform bodywork for their delivery vehicles and so, much sheeting and roping had to take place during journeys involving many drops. The Lacon name dates back to the 18th century and the company remained a family concern until the 1950s.

Left: Unusual in brewery fleets anywhere in the country, were the three Latil tractors employed at Chiswell Street for hauling trailer tanks to the London area bottling stores. Based on French design the tractors had drive, steering and braking on all four wheels, features which made them eminently suitable for handling trailers in confined spaces. The three machines dated from 1928, 1935 and 1936 and remained in use until 1947 when they were sold, the two later machines going to T.M. Fairclough Sons who employed a large number of the Latil tractors hauling insulated meat containers from the docks to Smithfield Market. One of the trio, L43 is pictured in early post-war days with bomb damaged buildings much in evidence.

Top right & middle right: Beer transport of a very unusual type was pressed into service in July 1944, when Spitfires of the 2nd Tactical Air Force were used to unofficially deliver casks of Strongs' bitter to the troops in Normandy during WWII. By adapting existing depth charge fittings below the wings of the 'planes, a special carrier listed as 'XXX Depth Charge Fitment' allowed for the wooden casks to be carried, one under each wing.

Bottom right: In more leisurely times the local carnival could be certain to attract quite a number of companies both local and national, who were keen to exploit the possibility of a captive audience for any publicity message they care to pronounce. Pictured in the yard at Britannia Street is a 1936 Dennis 45-cwt vehicle from the nearby Weston Rise depot carefully decorated to impart the cleanliness and charm of the Whitbread 'local'. A section of bar counter complete with a couple of beer pumps and pin of bitter suitably covered, is backed up with the almost regulation stuffed prize fish in glass case, and one of the attractive circular cast iron pub tables. A number of vehicle headlamps and fog lamps are provided to throw light on the display, while some floral edging reminds everyone that it is summer!

Left: During the 1930s beer in bulk for th[e] bottling stores was handled by a fleet of 2[0-] barrel and 40-barrel tanks mounted on bo[th] rigid and trailer type vehicles. This diminuti[ve] Albion is of 20-barrel capacity, dating fro[m] 1936 although photographed in 1946. It is [of] course petrol engined, has a fixed startin[g] handle, no nearside mirror, and the headligh[ts] are barely larger than the sidelights! This w[as] at the time when the vehicles were given pref[ix] letters to denote the make, so with A for Albi[on] the new AECs had to be prefixed Ae and th[e] Austins Au.

Below: The loading facilities of Weston Ris[e,] seen in this 1947 view, were typical of those [at] the majority of depots, where vehicles we[re] reversed up to the loading bank and the cas[es] taken from sack barrows or trolleys hand load[ed] from stacks on the bank or from conveyo[rs] from the cellar storage. The little Comm[er] being loaded was not a typical vehicle in t[he] fleet, most being 3-ton or 5-ton Denn[is] machines and one can just be seen furth[er] along the loading bank.

Right: The Phoenix Brewery at Wateringbury was established by Frederick Leney & Sons Ltd. and they acquired three other small breweries in various parts of Kent before being absorbed into the House of Whitbread in 1927. Vehicles continued to carry the Leney name on the cab doors, in much the same way as the depot vehicles were lettered, and the brewery premises retained much of the atmosphere associated with local country breweries. Vehicles operated over the years included AEC and Albion types, but local industry was also supported by the purchase of this Vulcan 6-tonner obtained from nearby Maidstone during 1946.

Below: Pictured against a background of blitzed buildings in the early days after the war, is this Thornycroft 'Nippy' 3-tonner parked outside the Silk Street garage of the brewery. This model represented the first batch of standard cask type vehicles in the post-war years at a time when most delivery vehicles were still petrol engined — note the fixed starting handle! The cab has been built specially deep in order to provide space for the delivery crew and the high-sided body is of the type maintained as standard for cask work for many years. Built wholly of hardwood, the body has steel reinforcement at the strategic points as well as wearing strips on the floor, the wide centre panel is in aluminium, and there is no side access to the load. A pair of steel bars retain the load at the rear, whilst another steel bar acts as a centre tie for the body sides.

Right: The modernisation of the Brewery fleet in post-war days began with the acquisition of 19 Dennis 'Pax' petrol engined delivery vehicles toward the end of 1946. These were followed by half-a-dozen Thornycroft HF model 'Nippy' 3-tonners and a similar number of Dennis 'Max' 7½-tonners, all being fitted with Marshall bodywork. One of the latter was shown on Stand 64 of Marshalls Flying School at the 1948 Commercial Motor Show at Earls Court, and the catalogue entry explains that it was a 14ft wheelbase chassis fitted with a body 17ft 9in long with 3ft 6in sides, and that the cab was panelled in aluminium and fitted with an illuminated headboard. One of this batch with Marshall bodywork and cab is shown here.

Above: The supply of new vehicles during wartime was severely curtailed, and when the need was proven the choice was limited. At the end of hostilities there were still shortages of steel which made for long delivery delays, and the efforts of the motor industry were directed toward export markets. The Vulcan 6PF was one of the vehicles that was available against MOWT permit for civilian use, and this early post-war example was delivered during 1945 to The Sheffield Free Brewery Co. Ltd. The company had a rather chequered career, passing into the control of others in 1954, to Tennant Brothers a year later and so to Whitbreads in 1961.

Below right: Fleet No.455 was the first of the post-war AEC 'Mammoth Major' eight wheel long distance vehicles to be purchased, and dates from 1947. It joined the four pre-war AEC four axle machines which had been acquired in 1937 and 1939 and which remained in service for a few more years. Following the standard Whitbread practice of the period, this vehicle represents the epitomy of the British trunk haulage unit of the early post-war era, being of maximum capacity, air-braked but limited to around 34 mph top speed. With bodywork and painting carried out by E.A. Turner of Kingston, this immaculate vehicle saw many years of service, running loads of bottled beer from Chiswick bottling depot to depots and outlets in the north, west and south of the country.

Below: The use of road haulage contractors for the transport of loads to the provincial depots had originated with the steam wagons as an alternative to using the railways. In some instances the work was of a casual nature, but when the work was on a regular basis both contractor and brewer gained from having vehicles painted in the company livery. The Maudslay 'Militant' shown here was a 40-barrel tanker used to augment the company owned vehicles used to ferry supplies of bulk beer from Chiswell Street brewery to any of the London or provincial bottling stores. The vehicle dates from 1945 and was part of a sizeable fleet on regular contract hire from C.D. & T. (Contracts) Ltd. who had a depot at Power Road, Chiswick close-by the Whitbread bottling store.

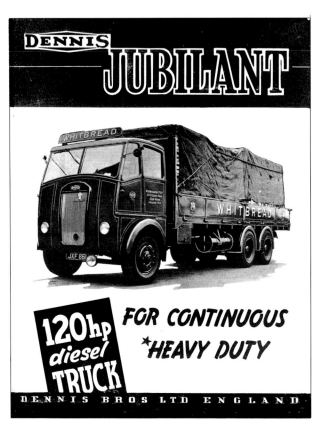

Top left: Based on the Austin 10 car chassis of the early post-war years, this van was used by the Advertising department and located at the Britannia Street offices. Typical of contemporary light van practice of the period it featured front-opening 'suicide' cab doors so easily damaged in windy weather, a fabric roof to prevent drumming, built-in direction indicators, a single bottom-mounted windscreen wiper, fairings or spats over the rear wheels and no front or rear bumpers. For an advertising vehicle the paint scheme of dark brown and black with plain lettering is hardly eye-catching, and the additional roof board although finished in post office red carried too long a message to provide rapid impact on any potential customers who might see it on its journey!

Right: In this 1947 photograph of Chiswell Street, one of the recently delivered Dennis 'Pax' 5-tonners is seen having just left the North Yard, the narrow entrance to which is just behind the vehicle cab. Soon, the building occupied by Eldrid, Ottoway & Co. was to be acquired and rebuilt with its frontage set back from the road, at the same time the gateway was widened to provide a much more open aspect to this part of the Chiswell Street premises. Just visible in the far distance is one of the Pickfords contract tankers which had just departed, probably loaded for Cardiff.

Middle left: In 1948 there was a slight change of vehicle buying policy when the first of a number of Maudslay 'Mogul' four wheelers were acquired. These replaced some of the older Dennis and Leyland 6-tonners for inter-depot work, and they still retained the old style of fixed-sided body although of more usual height. The vehicle shown was the fourth of a batch of ten and was allocated to the main bottling store at Grays Inn Road, which was opposite the Britannia Street offices. In later years some of the Maudslays had flat bodies mounted as the change to forklift truck load handling took place.

Bottom left: In the early post-war years Dennis Brothers introduced a rigid six wheel chassis to their range — the 'Jubilant'. Whitbreads duly tried a handful of them for long distance trunking operations, and the first of them, Fleet No. 445 entered service toward the middle of 1947. Powered by Dennis's own six cylinder, direct-injection diesel engine of 8 litres capacity, drive was by means of a dry two-plate clutch to a five speed overdrive gearbox. The rear bogie was of the double drive type with overhead worm gears and three differentials to equalise the drive. Dennis Brothers again used a photograph of one of the fleet, No. 468 on the sales brochure for the model, and it is interesting to note that by this date (1947), they were using the American idiom of truck as against the accepted term of lorry.

Right: For many years the contract fleet supplied by C.D. & T. (Contracts) Ltd. was largely made up of Scammell rigid eight-wheelers complete with the approved type of fixed body sides and employing the tailored load sheet with webbing straps. A number of new vehicles were in the course of being delivered when the company was nationalised in 1948 so some were delivered with the new company name of C.D. & T. (Contracts) BTC Ltd. as shown in this photograph. Note the mixture of tyre equipment used on the vehicles. The rear bogie, which has rubber suspension, has 14.00x20 singles instead of the twin tyres which were optional on this model.

Left: A view of the Silk Street garage at Chiswell Street looking toward the two roller shutters which faced Whitecross Street. To the left, one of the old electrics can just be seen with the solid tailboard hinged down. At centre is Au49 a wartime Austin with 20-barrel tank, while at right is a 1929-registered Latil four wheel drive tractor (L50), which was obtained second-hand.

Top right: The rapid expansion of brewery fleets in the decade or so following World War II was matched by a considerable increase in the fortunes of Dennis Brothers of Guildford. Their 'Pax' range of 3- and 5-ton chassis gained them many brewery customers, particularly in the south of England. The front cover of the 1948 Dennis sales brochure featured this rather tranquil scene of a delivery to a Fremlins house by one of their 5-ton 'Pax' lorries, and surprisingly the vehicle does not dominate the picture. Power for this model came from the makers own four-cylinder side-valve petrol engine of 100x120mm dimensions which produced 70bhp and drove through a single plate clutch and four speed gearbox to a spiral bevel gear rear axle.

Middle right: This Austin 3-tonner is shown in the livery of Chislehurst Mineral Waters shortly after the company had been acquired. Soon to become the production facility for the newly-created Chandy Bottling Company, the fleet was modernised and extended for an expansion into a market that some thirty years later was to become known as low-alcohol drinks. Note how very deep body runners have had to be incorporated in order to raise the body floor to the height of a loading bank — in direct contrast to the vehicles of today, where everything is done to achieve a low loading height.

Bottom right: The increased trade of the early post-war years brought greater demand for the means of transport through the fleet. The traffic in bulk beer from brewery to bottling stores had been handled by a small fleet of rigid tankers on Saurer, Albion and Austin chassis, plus a few trailer tanks with Latil tractors, and a decision was made to make the switch to articulated vehicles in order to achieve greater flexibility as well as providing a quicker turnround of the equipment. A handful of Dennis 'Horla' tractors were acquired, and the old pre-war trailer tanks converted to Scammell automatic-coupling articulated operation. In this 1950 photograph H2 is shown coupled to C2 outside the tanker unloading bay of Grays Inn Road bottling plant. The tank is of the old unlagged type and has been mounted on a carrier frame with a single axle having odd-sized tyre equipment. Later new articulated tanks were fully insulated, were of the frameless type and had wheel and tyre equipment to match the tractor units.

Left: In 1945 the Cheltenham Original Brewery Co. Ltd. merged with the Hereford & Tredegar Brewery Ltd. to form Cheltenham & Hereford Breweries Ltd. This company later merged with the Stroud Brewery Co. Ltd. to form West Country Brewery Holdings Ltd. which came under Whitbread control in 1963. This example of the C.H.B. fleet is one of their Sentinel diesel types with platform bodywork, and dates from 1948. With its underfloor engine layout, the Sentinel was quite popular in brewery fleets, for its roomy cab was capable of accommodating a three-man crew in comfort, although the shape of the sliding door was not conducive for rapid exit from the cab. The other attribute of this vehicle was the ease of engine accessibility by virtue of its horizontal position to the rear of the cab with the cylinder heads to the offside.

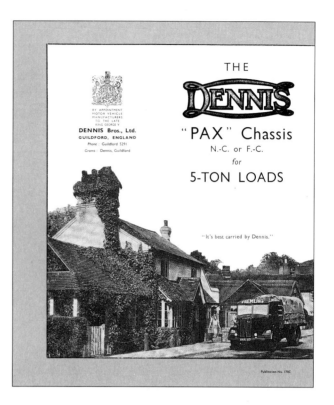

THE
DENNIS
"PAX" Chassis
N.-C. or F.-C.
for
5-TON LOADS

"It's best carried by Dennis."

DENNIS Bros., Ltd.
GUILDFORD, ENGLAND

Left: One of the less glamorous activities of bulk beer delivery was never-the-less one of the most interesting technically — the road/rail tank fleet. In 1931 the use of a road tanker which could be quickly mounted on a railway wagon for speedy long-distance transport, was pioneered through the joint efforts of the Southern Railway, R.A. Dyson the trailer builders, and the Co-operative Dairies concern. Having proved the concept, it was extended to other operators including Whitbread & Co. who had several of the tanks operating over various sections of the rail network. In this photograph one of the 40-barrel tanks is seen at Chiswell Street prior to being towed to Camden goods depot by the B.R. Latil tractor. At Camden the tank would be shunted aboard a vacuum-braked flat wagon for the overnight run to Glasgow behind an express train, ready for morning delivery to the depot. The trailer tanks featured vacuum braking, Ackermann type steering, massive lashing rings and a rear towing bracket so that they could be towed in tandem when empty.

Below: In the early 1950s British Road Services replaced some of the Scammell 'rigid eights' on the Whitbread contract with a new fleet of Leyland 'Octopus' and Foden FG model rigid eight-wheel chassis. This photograph shows one of the Fodens, and it could fairly be said to epitomise the long-distance bulk fleet of the day. The Whitbread style of fixed sided body with internal load fixings is retained, and the fitted sheet with its leather straps and buckles for tidiness, and the 2" wide webbing security straps which retain the load both transversely and longitudinally, are clearly visible. Note the recessed Lucas trafficators on the cab quarter panel and the four chromium-plated hinged steps to the rear of the nearside door.

Right: Many companies attempted to gain some publicity from the Festival of Britain Exhibition which opened on the south bank site in May 1951. Whitbreads had a Dennis 'Pax' fitted with this special box type sign on the cab roof in order to publicise the fact that Whitbread beers were available at the Festival Gardens site. The vehicle was part of the fleet at Lewisham depot which served the part of south London where the Battersea Fun Fair and Pleasure Gardens was located, some little way upstream from the actual Festival of Britain site.

Below: A late 1940s scene at the Middle Stage of Chiswell Street, with a mixture of local delivery vehicles in evidence. Three of the newly-acquired Dennis 'Pax' fleet are on the left with a Swiss-built Saurer at the far end. Just visible are the cabs of two of the GV electric lorries, while another example has just appeared under the sundial. To the right of the picture a pair of horses enjoy a meal break outside the draymen's lobby.

Left: It is quite commonplace to find telephones in the cabs of modern commercial vehicles, but back in the 1950s any such installation was decidedly pioneer. Experiments with such a scheme were tried out at Newcastle-on-Tyne depot in 1952 using Pye equipment installed in one of the Dennis 'Pax' delivery vehicles. This photograph which shows the equipment in use, also provides a good view of a lorry cab interior of the period, with its very simple controls and meagre instruments, although it did feature fully opening windscreens. Back at the depot a large scale plan of the area covered was used to trace the progress of the vehicle, with the aid of a Dinkytoy model lorry!

Top right: As well as using the Dennis 'Pax' chassis for local delivery work a number of the shorter wheelbase 'Horla' type were acquired for use as both drawbar and articulated tractor units. Used mainly for the shuttle journeys to the London area bottling stores at Chiswick, Grays Inn Road, Lewisham and Tottenham, the fleet of 40-barrel tanks were used in the best of Scammell-coupling tradition by continual coupling and uncoupling at both the Chiswell Street brewery and bottling depot ends of the runs. Note that this tractor is numbered H12A — 13 was never used in the fleet numbering system!

Middle left: Smallest of the Seddon range was the 25-cwt van fitted with the Perkins three cylinder P3 diesel engine. In July 1954 three of these vans were purchased for the Chandy Bottling Co. fleet, and fitted with special bodywork by Express Motor Bodies incorporating a lift-up flap on the nearside, which revealed a counter for the dispensing of drinks. The vans were used at open-air events and sales drives. Within a couple of years the policy regarding Chandy changed; two of the vans being repainted in other company liveries and the third sold off.

Right: As the Dennis 'Horla' tractors of the brewery fleet began to age they were replaced by Seddon Mark V tractor units, and S85 was the first of these, entering service in 1954. Originally purchased for the regular shuttle runs from Chiswell Street brewery to the London area bottling depots at Chiswick, Lewisham, Tottenham and Grays Inn Road with the 40-barrel tanks, they were later used for longer journeys as the first of the 10-ton cask semi-trailers were brought into service to supplant the rigid vehicles used hitherto for deliveries to provincial depots.

Above: In common with many other road transport operators, the company bottling stores fleet added its first articulated vehicles during the 1950s with a number of 10-ton payload outfits. Employing the Dennis 'Horla' tractor unit, which was a short wheel-base version of the normal control 'Pax' chassis, fitted with the Scammell type of automatic coupling and using Scammell semi-trailers with low drop-side bodies, the vehicles were mainly employed on inter-depot transfer work.

Above: In 1956 a new contract was agreed between Whitbread & Co. and J. Spurling Ltd. for the supply of two articulated vehicles for use on the long distance deliveries of cask beer to certain provincial depots. Under Whitbread guidance a pair of Seddon Mk 14 tractors with Gardner engines were acquired and they were even numbered S117 and S142 in the brewery fleet, just to confuse everyone! With two regular drivers they were employed on a tight schedule to places such as Bristol, Cardiff, Exeter, Plymouth as well as Liverpool and Birkenhead as shown by the trailer boards in this photograph. The vehicles did not behave well, were not liked by the drivers and were later replaced with more orthodox Ford units.

Top left: During the 1950s the fleet operated by Strong & Co. of Romsey, Hants included Albion, Bedford, Leyland, Morris, Scammell and Thornycroft types and numbered about 40 in all. In addition to providing a delivery service to houses, hotels, clubs and off-licences some of the fleet was engaged in supplying certain beers to two smaller breweries, Wethereds at Marlow and Higgs located in Reading who had been acquired in 1949 and 1953 respectively. This photograph shows one of the dozen Leyland 'Comet' 7-tonners with a Tasker 5-ton trailer, which has just returned from Wethereds with a full load of empty cases.

Left: Despite the very reliable service provided by the early post-war fleet of AEC 'Mammoth Major' 80-barrel tanks, during 1956 an initial batch of three Atkinson LI586A eight-wheel chassis were acquired as the basis for three new Burnett & Rolfe 80-barrel tanks, or vessels as the engineers liked to call them. Something of a compromise was made however, for they came with the AEC 9.6-litre engine fitted, presumably to limit the amount of spares it was necessary to carry. This vehicle, At89, was the third of the trio, and was finished in the current Mackeson livery of black and silver with a white panel carrying the name in black shaded in silver. Note that the detachable destination boards carried on the tank sides use the name Mackeson's Stout which was the title used up to this period when the change to a singular name-style was adopted.

Above: Yes, what is it? With a specialist cab supplied by the bodybuilders this Austin 5-tonner was one of a pair put into service for the Chandy Bottling Co. in 1954. In trying to achieve a low platform height a compromise has had to be made by providing boxes over the rear wheels, necessary because of the 750x20 size tyres. Extremely high head- and tail-boards are used in the design and the two are strengthened by means of a centre nameboard and a pair of steel tiebars. The body floor is slightly lower at the centre in order to stabilise the load, and even the wheelboxes are provided with inward tapering bearers to help in this respect.

Left: Although the Chandy Bottling Co's fleet was small by comparison with the beer delivery fleet of the parent company, it did contain some unusual types. As well as a bonneted three-cylinder diesel-engined Seddon, this Austin 15-cwt van formed part of the delivery fleet. Based on the FX3 taxi-cab chassis of the period, it was powered by the makers four cylinder petrol engine, rendering it quite fast and of course highly manoeuverable with its small turning circle.

Middle left: Described by some as the epitomy of long distance operation, the AEC 'Mammoth Major' 80-barrel tanks with their 40-barrel drawbar trailers, marked a peak in the company's transport operations which is difficult to surpass. Pictured heading up Holloway Road on a July evening in 1956, Ae83 and its trailer are on the way to Ashton-under-Lyne bottling depot with one of the many loads carried each week during the summer season. In those pre-motorway days Ashton-under-Lyne was 11 hours driving from London. A number of the AECs were permanently taxed for trailer operation, although the need for them varied at different times of the year.

Below: Nostalgic Saturday photograph of the 'Snake Pit' vehicle parking area at Chiswell Street in the late 1950s, with no less than seven AEC and Atkinson 80-barrel tanks, five 40-barrel articulated tanks, plus a Dennis 'Horla' yard shunter and the Bedford 30-cwt van for the Builders department. All these tanks would have been empty, any tanks loaded ready for a journey would have been left adjacent to the tank loading points in either the North or South yards.

Right: On several occasions the transport operations of the company have been featured in the trade press, and one such occasion was in the 1950s when a night journey from London to Cardiff by tanker was reported in an article entitled 'Operation Beer'. One of the photographs used to illustrate the article was this evocative shot of the AEC 'Mammoth Major' Ae56 as it paused in Newport en route to the bottling store at Cardiff.

Below: Not all brewery vehicles are used for the beer delivery; a few perform duties which are very necessary although less glamorous than the majority of the fleet. This Seddon tipper was one such vehicle, being employed by Chiswell Street Building department as a 'maid of all work' performing tasks such as clearing rubbish from closed houses, delivering materials for house refurbishment, and collecting supplies of building materials. It was particularly useful for the erection of new inn sign posts: the post would be carried on the body and then gently tipped into the hole dug for it, and the ground tamped down to maintain it in the upright position. The vehicle was photographed in King Square, EC1, an area useful for vehicle photography with few parked cars and room to manoeuvre large vehicles.

Left: This AEC Mark III 'Mammoth Major' represents the long distance vehicle of the bottling stores fleet as the change to palletised loads took place in the late 1950s. A flat body with deep side raves has replaced the earlier style of fixed sided body, but load security is still maintained by webbing straps fixed to points at the edge of the floor so as not to obstruct the name on the side of the panels. The extremely high slatted headboard carries a small sheet rack, while a larger area is available on the cab roof and the old style semaphore indicators can just be made out positioned in line with the rear view mirrors, which appear tiny by today's standards.

Top right: Bentley's Yorkshire Breweries Ltd. took delivery of this 7-ton Commer in May 1961, it being one of 25 vehicles supplied by Lister & Edmond of York. The chassis had to be specially extended to 13ft 6in by Baico Ltd. in order to accommodate a 24ft body, which is fitted with 5ft high detachable steel stanchions and a double row of chains. A box is provided on the nearside to carry lowering hook and barrel rope for cask work.

Middle right: Unlike any of the other Atkinson four axle chassis, At138 sported an all-aluminium tipping hopper body for the transport of malt in bulk. It was employed on collecting malt from the maltings at King's Lynn or Dereham in Norfolk on a daily basis and returning to Chiswell Street brewery. A special high-ratio drive axle made it eminently suitable for the long round trip which was carried out on a tight schedule.

Bottom right: An early stage in cellar tank development was the use of an open vehicle with small tanks bolted on in a temporary fashion. This 1957 photograph shows an ex Whitbread Dennis 'Max' delivery vehicle in the course of being adapted for bulk beer delivery by Norman & Pring of Exeter. The two 10-barrel tanks have been bolted to a pair of stout timbers and arranged with their outlet cocks facing inward. The engineer is presently arranging a system of piping and valves to bring the two outlets together on the nearside of the vehicle, prior to making the connection to the loading main at the brewery.

Left: Pictured in the vehicle park to the north of Chiswell Street is this Atkinson articulated vehicle loaded with four of the 20-barrel Transportable Beer Tanks (TBTs). These tanks were used to supplement the regular bulk road tank fleet at peak times, as well as being the replacements for the trade which had previously been carried in wooden hogsheads, and which were transported by boat across the channel to Belgium or by coaster to Scotland. In this photograph the tanks are actually being recalibrated by the brewery engineers for HM Customs, and the officially approved 1-barrel measure can be seen on the walkway.

Left: The 1964 Construction & U
Regulations were instrumental in Denn
Brothers introducing their 'Maxim' range
four and six wheelers which embodied
Cummins V8 diesel engine. Whitbre
acquired a number of the 9ft 6in wheelba
tractor units but they proved difficult
operation. The engine developed 185b
from its 7.7 litre capacity and torque peak
at some 1750 rpm. To get the best out of t
engine it required to be driven at mu
higher 'revs' than those of the old in-li
engines. Some of the younger drivers fou
this to their liking but the older drivers we
reticent to take the engine to its maximu
'revs' and its performance suffered according

Right: The impressive lines of the Atkinson 80-barrel tank are evident in this candid shot of At167 which entered service in the autumn of 1960. One of two such vehicles, they were the first of the Atkinson L1786X type chassis in the company fleet featuring the Gardner LX type engine rated at 150bhp. A nice period touch is given by the handcart, a three wheel type much used by the local road-sweepers.

Middle right: Pictured south-bound on the M1 motorway after loading at Oakley Road, Luton is one of a pair of D-Series Ford tractor units which were supplied on contract hire by J. Spurling Ltd., a member of the Transport Development Group. Spurlings also operated other vehicles on casual work for the brewery at Chiswell Street using both company and their own trailers The two Ford tractors and their drivers later passed to the control of Whitbread & Co.

Below left: This line-up for the Archibald Campbell, Hope and King fleet shows, that in true Scottish tradition, they were users of the Glasgow-built Albion marque, with a new style 'Claymore' enjoying pole position, while the five vehicles furthest from the camera are heavier type ERF chassis.

Below: Photographed at night at the Luton brewery is one of a pair of AEC Mark V 'Mammoth Major' tankers which were originally placed in service with platform bodies for depot deliveries of bottled beer. With the gradual change to articulated vehicles for long distance deliveries the maximum capacity rigids were declared obsolete rendering a change to tank operation preferable to disposal.

Left: One of the problems encountered when using a lorry sheet to merely cover the load, is that any roping over the sheet to secure it can result in damage to the cases by the force exerted as the ropes are tightened by the use of a 'dolly' type of knot. One method of alleviating the problem was to encourage drivers to place boards or plastic angles at the top corners of the load and rope over these to spread the tension. Another system tried was to use a webbing strap with normal rope ends so that it could be attached to the rope hooks in the usual way. Pictured here is one of the Seddon Mk.10 vehicles of Tennant Brothers Ltd. of Sheffield, loaded with about 10-tons of half-pints in wooden boxes secured with webbing straps.

Below: Amongst the many Bedford TK and Ford D-series operated during the 1970s were a small batch of Dodge G-series trucks acquired with standard Boalloy Tautliner bodies for local delivery work. With the second generation of the Hi-Line cab, the chassis type was a follow-on from the earlier Commer range, emanating from the Dunstable works, later to become part of the Renault empire. The vehicles were disposed of during the fleet replacement scheme with the introduction of the larger size pallet.

Right: The use of bulk beer tanks installed in the cellars of houses and clubs is more prevalent in the north of the country, particularly where the trade is concentrated in towns with high density housing, or heavy industry with the attendant working-mens clubs. Such is the demand, that in the height of the season one customer could take up to 150 barrels of beer in a week! To meet such demands vehicles of large capacity are required, such as the Seddon articulated outfit shown here. Based on a plain platform semi-trailer, the unit has ten 5-barrel demountable tanks securely attached to the trailer floor, with all the tanks on each side being connected to one delivery pipe which in turn is connected to the delivery pump and metering equipment carried in the enclosed compartment at the rear. Each of the tanks is fitted with piping and gauges for the supply of CO_2 which is applied to the top of the tank to assist with the discharge and prevent 'fobbing'.

Below: Tinsley Workshop with a variety of 1970s vehicles. On the left is an 18-ton gcw Seddon tractor with Perkins 6.354 engine, coupled to a York tandem axle semi-trailer. Next is a 1978 Dodge G15 model local delivery vehicle also with Perkins 6.354 engine, and Boalloy Tautliner bodywork. In the foreground is one of the Ford Escort vans used by the Cellar Service departments, whilst behind it on the Laycock screw type vehicle lift are a pair of twin-steer Bedford TKs. Next can be seen a rear view of one of the 50-barrel bulk beer tankers enclosed in van style bodywork and lettered in Whitbread Trophy livery, whilst to the right of the picture is one of the then current fleet of ERF B-series 32-ton gcw tractor for long distance primary deliveries.

Left: In an attempt to progress from a plain platform body with sheets and ropes for security, a large number of Bedford TK twin-steers were fitted with this style of wire and post bodywork. In what seemed a good idea at the time, the six horizontal wires along each side could be detached from either end for loading and the intermediate posts removed for fork truck access. With posts replaced and wires attached, the hand ratchet mechanism visible at the lower forward part of the body was used to tension the cables, so retaining the load. So great was the force exerted by the ratchet, that some strong-arm draymen could easily wind-up the cables so as to make them like the strings on a harp, and the vertical posts would be permanently canted inwards.

Top right: In 1974 this model 608 Mercedes Benz was acquired as a development vehicle and allocated to Hornsey depot for handling small deliveries to city centre accounts where access was difficult. Equipped with a plain flat body 2.5m wide which could accommodate the new large pallets, the vehicle was later transferred to Luton and finally finished its operational life at Sheffield in the 1980s.

Middle right: A normal height Volvo FL617 chassis forms the basis of this box van which entered service in March 1988 for the Thresher off-licence and wine merchant delivery service. The livery adopted is similar to that used on the shops nationwide in order to be readily identified as a house style as opposed to the brand names currently being used for the beer delivery fleet.

Bottom right: In the early 1970s the company started to use the large area presented by the tailboards of the largest trailers as a travelling billboard for advertising various beers. The first to be presented was Gold Label with the message — "Strong as a double scotch — Less than half the price", and this was really the start of using vehicles to publicise brand names.

Left: The first purpose-built drop frame low loader was this DAF 2100 delivered in 1984. Using the current standard chassis suitably modified by DAF at Colchester, it was fitted with a Boalloy Curtainsider body which had centre posts to maintain rigidity, and the CO_2 cylinders were carried in a separate compartment at the front of the floor. The compartment behind the cab is merely to panel-in the section over the gearbox. Just ten of this original type were used in the fleet.

BELGIUM & EXPORTS

T he company opened its first Belgium depot in Brussels in 1904, followed in 1906 by one in Antwerp. In 1908 the Brussels facility moved to new premises, in 1910 Liege depot was opened, Ghent opened in 1913 and in 1914 Antwerp depot moved to new premises.

As will be understood, the Great War of 1914-1918 played havoc with the company's Belgian operations and the continental depots took some time in getting back to normal after The Armistice was signed.

Transport in the early days centred around horse and mule vans for local deliveries, although there are records of motor vehicles being used before 1914. In true Whitbread tradition the Dennis lorry was used in Belgium, the first recorded being No.45 a 3½-ton Subsidy chassis delivered in 1920, it being joined by No.47 a similar vehicle shortly after.

The following year saw a Saurer 3-ton model 3AC go into service, and there may have been more, for the early records of the fleet are incomplete. Later acquisitions included a couple of 2-ton Chevrolets in 1928, a model RC35 3-ton Brossel Freres in 1929, followed by a couple of model A Fords.

The 1930s saw Bovy, Ford, Morris and Chevrolet trucks added, and by the outbreak of WWII Chevrolets made up the greater part of the fleet. Records show that 16 of the Belgian fleet were commandeered in 1939, from a 1921 Bovy to a 1939 Chevrolet.

The post-war fleet kicked off with a handful of new Austins in 10cwt, 3-ton and 5-ton capacities, these later being joined by the LD vans, 3-Way models, Bedford S-type articulated, BMC 7-tonners, AEC Mandator and the rare normal control Seddon artic amongst others.

Trade to the Belgian market had been in cask beer originally but was later augmented by bottled beer, it eventually being bottled in Belgium with bulk supplies coming from London by way of casks brought by sea, but in the post-war years the demand grew at such a pace that plans were made to ship the beer over in bulk. This was achieved firstly by using 20-barrel transportable tanks which could be craned on and off ships plying between London Docks and Belgian ports. A second system was to use the jointly-owned road/rail tanks which were loaded at

DEPOT DE LA BRASSERIE WHITBREAD

Chiswell Street, taken to Mile End BR by road, shunted aboard a railway wagon, taken to Harwich by train and then run onto the BR ferry to Zeebrugge for onward transport to Brussels.

In May 1954 the first direct road journey took place with an AEC 80-barrel tank making the journey from London to Brussels by way of the British Railways cross-channel ferry from Dover to Dunkirk. This marked the start of an ever-increasing trade which expanded over the years by the addition of many more tankers as well as using another ferry service plying between Tilbury and Antwerp, articulated tanks also being used, with contractors supplying the tractors at either end of the journey.

Above right: One of the earliest Belgian vehicle photographs discovered is of this pre-Great War van complete with crew. The vehicle is a Bovy, produced by S.A. des Automobiles Industriels Bovy of Brussels-Molenbeek from early in the first decade of the century up to 1930 when they were acquired by Brossel. The body style is typical of the early motor bodies which closely followed older horse vehicle designs in having the lower part of the body within the rear wheels, with the upper part wider. Note the regular use of the roof for empties.

Above: Delivered to the Brussels depot in 1920 this 3½-ton Dennis was unusual in the fleet being a plain dropside lorry as opposed to the white-topped covered vans which gave a much more high class appearance for city delivery work. In this photograph of Fleet No. 45, 'Le Chauffeur' poses in his leather jacket and gaiters while a rather juvenile drayman hands down a case to the waiting trader who is complete with money bag. The load appears to be a mixture of local trade cases and export type boxes.

Left: A fine panoramic picture of what is probably the whole of Brussels depot staff and vehicles. In the forefront the staff have been assembled on top of a pair of flat horse drays and as the vista spreads there are seven pair-horse covered vans, although some pairs could be mules. Next come a pair of model A Ford vans while the outer ends of the display show four Dennis vans which form the heaviest part of the delivery fleet. The date is probably around 1930.

Left: This period view of the depot at Brussels shows that in the 1920s the majority of the fleet was either mule- or horse-drawn, with the motor vehicle just beginning to appear. The fleet colours at this time would appear to be green lower parts with white or cream for the canvas or boarded tilt covers. Worthy of note is the fact that the two horse-drawn vehicles in the foreground have cabs for the crew, a feature which never extended to the British part of the company fleet!

Top right: In 1929 the company acquired this 3-ton model RC35 Brossel for operation from the depot at Brussels, and as it turned out it was to be the last genuine Belgian vehicle to be bought for the next ten years. In the years which followed the fleet was gradually updated with a number of Chevrolets, until just at the outbreak of WWII a couple of Bovy 2-tonners were acquired, only to be swiftly commandeered by the military.

Middle right: Fleet No. 285 was the second of a pair of 3-ton Chevrolets which were acquired during 1935 for operation in the Belgian branch of the business. Several American medium-weight truck lines were being sold in mainland Europe at this time, and Whitbread had already tried a few of the Ford model A trucks for delivery work from its Belgian depots. The lower part of the bodywork on this vehicle has the unusual treatment of having imitation wood-graining, but the upper part has the more orthodox white canvas stretched over a wooden frame.

Bottom right: Allocated to the company depot at Antwerp in 1951, this 25cwt capacity van is a standard production Austin of the 'Three Way' type, the name being adopted because of the facility of easy access to both sides and the rear. The vehicles were particularly prone to skidding when unladen over the Belgian cobbles, because of the engine being positioned forward of the front axle.

Left: The Transport Department of the Bottling Stores located at Britannia Street near Kings Cross, was responsible for the fleet of vehicles in Belgium, so it naturally followed similar lines to those used in Britain, except that vehicles were obtained locally. In pre-war days the Belgium fleet was mostly American Chevrolets plus a couple of Belgian-built Bovy light trucks, most of which were quickly impressed by the military authorities during the war. With no Dennis representation in Belgium the company chose to use the Austin marque in the early post-war days, and this K4 Austin is shown as put into service in 1948.

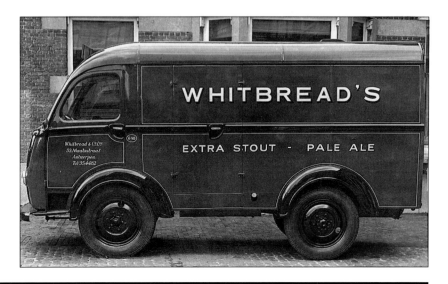

Above: Following the widespread use of various Seddon models in the brewery fleet, a heavy version was tried as a replacement for the AEC units currently in use in 1960 in the Belgian operation. This is one of the unusual bonneted Mark 12 models used in combination with an equally unusual semi-trailer of local manufacture, which displays an amazing complex design for something as simple as a semi-trailer for bottled beer. For well over a decade Seddon enjoyed considerable sales in Belgium through the enterprise of the local agents Hocke.

Below: With a final polish and the tyres blackened, Ae19 poses for photographs just before the commencement of the regular service of carrying beer in bulk to the Whitbread depot in Brussels in May 1954. This new service, using the cross-channel ferries of British Railways was well publicised, for although it was by no means the first time the train ferry had been used by commercial vehicles, it did establish a new service on a regular basis. Luckily, Whitbread had been a customer of the railways for a very long time, so negotiations for the use of the ferry were comparatively smooth.

Above: The first ships used for the roll-on, roll-off bulk movements across the English Channel were those of British Railways which had been built for the cross-channel rail services. Within a short while Frank Bustard started his service across the channel using ex-wartime tank landing craft, duly followed a few years later by a number of vessels specially designed for the expanding road vehicle movements into the European mainland. The Empire Baltic was one of the ships provided for this service which ran from Tilbury to Antwerp, and Whitbreads took advantage of this alternative to the BR service on a regular basis.

Below: A sight never to be repeated — a street full of rigid eight-wheel tankers! At the height of the season there might be up to 1000-barrels of beer being consigned to Belgium, and at one period it could have been in rigid tanks, articulated tanks and in demountable tanks according to the availability of tank capacity. The drivers engaged on this prestigious service for the company were specially selected from long-serving drivers at Chiswell Street, and although it appeared rather glamorous in those days of pioneering cross-channel road transport, doing two trips a week in high summer could mean little time at home.

Above: With his vehicle polished to perfection, driver Henry Anderson reverses Ae19 on to the train deck of the British Railways cross-channel train ferry at Dover's Western Docks on the occasion of the inaugural direct delivery to Belgium in May 1954. The next 20 years would witness a tremendous increase in this traffic to mainland Europe, the cross-channel service was also instrumental in achieving further economies in distribution costs, with some tankers returning from Europe with loads of wine.

Above: The first leg of the journey from Chiswell Street to Wateringbury, took the tankers through the heart of the City and across the River Thames by way of historic Tower Bridge. In this mid-morning scene in 1969 one of the Atkinson tankers heads south across the river admired by two small boys. The livery of this period was dark brown with a red panel and with Whitbread in white. The old illuminated headboards were replaced with a curved metal panel round the cab roof line with the company name flanked by a pair of tankards.

Above: Up, up and away! No, not an export of a vehicle complete with its load, but just a routine delivery by the Ship's Stores department to one of HM Ships in Portsmouth dockyard. With an aircraft carrier taking such large quantities of beer for a tour of duty, the easiest way of getting it aboard is to hoist the loaded vehicle up onto the deck. From here it is driven on to the aircraft lift, lowered down to the hangar deck and then driven to the mess store for unloading in the usual way.

Below: As the time came for the older AEC 80-barrel tanks to be replaced in the 1960s, the choice had been for the Atkinson L1786X chassis to be acquired. However, with Seddon keen to get their new DD8 model into the large fleets a decision was made to try the new model, and two chassis were ordered. The first, S171 was allocated to continental work, and the tiny circular AEC badge on the radiator grille indicates that Whitbread were still specifying that makers power unit in preference to the standard Gardner engine.

Right: Sparkling in the midday sunshine, Atkinson 80-barrel tanker At1200 stands poised on eight delicate Wedgwood bone china coffee cups in a square in Brussels in 1965. The occasion was a 'British Week' in the Belgian capital where extra emphasis was given to exports from Britain. Wedgwood approached Whitbread with the idea for this joint display and the author was despatched across the Channel to complete the delicate operation. Local staff from Brussels depot assisted with the jacking operation and the vehicle stood in this position for two weeks. The only casualties suffered were two cups broken — by vandals curious to see if they were filled with concrete!

Right: In 1965 the Publicity department thought it a good idea to send an initial load of Whitbread beers to the Britannia Inn which had been established at Milan in Italy. Anxious to achieve additional publicity for the journey, the vehicle also carried a giant size Whitbread Tankard fabricated from glass fibre which was duly manhandled on to the front of the Dennis six-wheeler chosen. The journey was routed through the recently completed Mont Blanc Tunnel in the hope of attracting press reportage, and one of the Brussels run drivers chosen for his experience. This cover photograph from the Transport Journal shows the vehicle and its load as it entered Italy from the Mont Blanc end of the tunnel.

Below: With the absence of a floating link between ship and shore, the variation in levels between the two often rendered vehicle loading on the Ro-Ro ferries rather hazardous. Here the first of the tilt-cab AEC 'Mandator' tractors is reversing the first of the new 120-barrel tanks aboard the cross-channel ferry at Tilbury in 1968. The amount of vertical articulation between tractor and trailer could cause problems with the airlines, and the landing legs need to be fully raised in order to clear the ramp.

WEIGHT, BULK & HEIGHT

In most transport functions there is a continual search for a more efficient way to carry the loads, and methods are under constant review in order to maximise on the equipment being used.

Beer transport is no exception, and over the years the vehicles, equipment, systems and planning have been subjected to frequent scrutiny in order to cut costs and improve the service provided. Brewers, engineers, management and operating staff have all had a part to play and the pace of change has quickened as the years have passed.

In the distant past someone must have decided that a four wheel waggon would carry more than the two wheel cart, and even if it did require another horse, the same two men could perform the deliveries. Then came mechanisation. The motor vehicle might have a greater original cost, but it didn't eat on Saturdays and Sundays when there were no deliveries to be made. In addition it took up less room to garage, and it probably fetched more at the end of a few years than the cats meat provided by a dead horse.

Development was certainly slow in the early days of the motor vehicle, for labour was cheap, and most brewers better employers than many other industries. As labour costs rose so did the need to make economies in any direction, provided the service did not suffer.

The most significant progress came with the desire to reduce vehicle unloading heights, especially with bottled beer which didn't roll along like a cask. True, the introduction of pallets and fork trucks helped cut down on handling, but that could usually only apply at the depot end of the journey. Various mechanical handling devices have been tried, with vehicles carrying their own small versions of the fork truck, or a vehicle mounted crane being tried.

But the easiest handling methods remain the simple ones, like having casks and kegs which can be rolled, and the modern version of the good old fashioned sack truck for packages which have corners. Faced with these limitations, the major area of attention remains the vehicle floor height, and to this end numerous modifications have been made.

A glance through the pages of this book reveals a wide variety of body styles — flat, flat with wheelboxes, dropside, slat or wire sided, posts and chains, box van, curtain sided, low loader, demountable, and all these just for deliveries without going into tankers, tippers, malt carriers etc.

So almost every conceivable type has been tried in order to provide the essentials of carrying the maximum amount possible, safely and securely, yet retaining ease and safe access for the loading and delivery of the contents.

In retrospect it is easy to criticise the old designs as being too high, not secure, poor access, slow unloading, unsafe for crews, poor public image, too short, insufficient capacity, etc. etc.

At one time there was little in the way of regulation to limit the wishes of the load planners, the capacity of vehicles was limited by what it could physically carry before it ground to a halt. Traffic density was light, speeds low, and urgency lower down the scale of priority.

Gradually the situation has changed, with vehicle legislation playing an ever increasing role in deciding vehicle design and layout. Lorries still have a wheel at each corner after all these years but almost everything else has changed, for there are limits on weight, length, wheelbase, overhang, width, speed, noise, smoke, braking, engine power, tyres, lighting and now height.

So transport engineers have had to arrange for a low loading height by means of a compromise, for the chassis frame has been lowered along the vehicle load area but remains at the previous height where the carrying axles are located. This is of little importance at the front axle which supports the cab and power unit, but at the rear axle the large diameter wheel/tyre combination prevents the floor from being lowered and this is one disadvantage which has to be admitted. The alternatives of front wheel drive and smaller wheels and tyres would still not resolve the problem entirely.

When looking at long distance vehicles the advantages of low height are not so important. With tankers the gain is in the area of greater stability, there being no problem with loading and unloading. The maximum capacity articulated outfits used for the primary function of depot deliveries also benefit little from lower loading heights save that of increased stability and safety.

Left: During the early post-war years the Bottling Stores fleet was expanded by the addition of large numbers of Dennis vehicles of three different model types — 'Pax, Max and Jubilant'. The Pax came in two sizes — 3-ton and 5-ton, and No. 486 pictured here in King Square was one of the smaller capacity. The bodywork is of the normal drop-side variety and the vehicle was finished in the Whitbread brown of the day with black wings, roof, chassis, fuel tank, wheels and mouldings. A gold-colour lining lightens and enhances the overall effect, and the company name on the body sides is flanked by the twin 'By Appointment' raised insignia of HM The King and HRH The Prince of Wales.

Left: With the importance of providing an adequate delivery service at the lowest unit cost, the search for economies in the distribution of the product is an on-going campaign. In the early 1960s a design of local delivery vehicle was made which embraced a larger vehicle in respect of body space and payload, than had been provided hitherto on a rigid chassis. Staying with the well tried Dennis marque, the rigid six-wheel Pax V (Mark 5) was chosen and the current Dennis advertisement reveals that a body space of 24 feet x 8 feet was achieved, while theoretically 12 tons could be handled. In practice the vehicle was of usual Dennis quality and the low loading height adequate for load handling, but the body space was of more use for sorting the load than the actual capacity. The single drive rear bogie had little articulation with the result that vehicles could lose traction on the slightest change of gradient which might occur at the entrance to a delivery point, and their traction on soft surfaces left a lot to be desired.

Top right: Detail photograph showing how a low loading customer delivery vehicle could be utilised to carry the tanks and equipment necessary for delivering bulk beer for cellar tank installations. The 5-barrel tanks are vertically mounted on a pair of rectangular tubes for handling by fork lift trucks, with the outlet cocks and CO_2 fittings to the front. All the pumps, gauges, connections, wiring and ancillary equipment is contained in the 'Dralinka' cabinet which is positioned on the wheelboxes. In service the side curtains would be drawn closed for cleanliness and appearance.

Below: Pictured at the western loading bay of Luton brewery is one of the large batch of Scammell 'Trunker' articulated outfits acquired for feeding cask, keg and bottled beers to distribution depots around the country. The special trailers had high headboards and tailboards with a yellow-coloured sheet attached to each, these being secured by webbing straps. Full loads were desirable, anything less being a problem, and pallets were often used to level-off the load or to fill any gaps. The tractor units were quite lightweight for the 32-ton weight category, but rather sluggish on the road when trying to pass holiday caravans for example.

Right: Reproduction of a York Trailer Co. advertisement from 1964 which shows the impressive frameless van semi-trailers that Flowers Breweries placed in service to replace a mixture of flat and smaller van artics used hitherto. Some of the vans were hand loaded by means of positioning roller conveyors in through the double rear doors, whilst others could be fork truck loaded at the rear and the pallets pushed forward by hand with the help of the Joloda system of having a pair of steel runners located in steel channels set into the floor.

Below: Fine action photograph of the Volvo F12 tractor unit coupled to a curtain-sided trailer fully loaded and being subjected to a high speed left-hand turn at MIRA in 1983. So great is the force exerted on the outfit that the nearside trailer wheels have lifted clear of the ground, and the anti-roll arm clamped to the trailer chassis is in contact with the road surface on the offside.

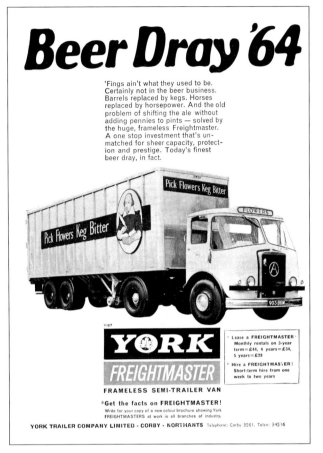

With pressure on the management to resist increases in crew numbers, the search for an ideal small delivery vehicle which would be suitable for handling deliveries to accounts with limited access has been approached in a variety of ways. Although almost 30 years separate the two vehicles shown here, there is still quite a similarity between them. The 7.5-tonne gvw MAN with curtain sides and roller shutter rear access *(left)*, has a design payload of 3.7-tonnes and is suitable for one-man operation. Introduced in 1987, the concept has recently been expanded by employing a six-wheel version of the type as shown on page 94, and a yet further exploitation of the idea is shown on page 96. *(Below)* During the 1960s several Karrier 'Gamecock' 4/5-ton payload vehicles were added to the bottling stores fleet for city deliveries. The rather cramped cab was suited to just two crew members and the open flat floor was actually lower toward its centre as an aid to load stability. Note how the top layers of these wooden boxes are strung to help keep the stack together, an alternative fixture being metal clips which were tried experimentally to connect adjacent boxes.

WHITBREAD NATIONWIDE

L ike every other brewer, Whitbread in its early history was primarily supplying customers that were close at hand, but gradually orders from further afield were found, and it is astonishing to discover that as early as 1745 there was a certain amount of export trade.

Records show that beer was being consigned to Gibraltar, Jamaica and New York soon after the business was started and the export business later extended to take in other parts of the USA as well as South Africa, India, Hong Kong, Australia and New Zealand.

Whitbread's first acquisition of another business was as early as 1812 when a small brewery at Lambeth was absorbed, but it was not until much later in the century when further acquisitions were made.

Beer was first put into bottles in 1868 and gradually this new trade brought about an expansion in the business by way of branches around the country. During the period 1891 to 1914 no fewer than 48 depots were opened, all because of the tremendous increase brought about by additional trade in bottled beer. It was said that well over 50% of the business was now in bottled beers.

During the period 1891-1902 Whitbread acquired five other breweries, and this helped the company to expand further. Sales were recorded in all parts of the country, and it was reported that there was scarcely a town or village where Whitbread bottled beers were not easily obtainable.

Naturally it was a side of the business that was easily copied by others, and the company could not rest on its laurels. The Great War intervened to halt further expansion for a few years, but with the restoration of peace in Europe, Whitbread was looking to expand further.

In 1920 the Notting Hill Brewery in West London was taken over, followed in 1923 by one at Forest Hill in South London. Against a background of falling trade 1927 saw the acquisition of Frederick Leney at Wateringbury in Kent, followed in 1929 by Jude, Hanbury, and Mackeson both of whom were located not far away.

There then followed a period of consolidation with no further mergers before WWII, but in the mid 1930s it was decided to try and expand the brand name market by a large advertising campaign for Mackeson Milk Stout.

In the early post-war years Flitton's Brewery in Bedfordshire was acquired in 1948, followed by Ameys of Petersfield in 1951 and Dales of Cambridge in 1955, all these gradually increasing the outlets for Whitbreads beers and spreading the name more nationwide.

It was during these mid 1950s that the new threat of take-overs from outside the industry started to make themselves apparent, and Whitbreads were

1961: Tennant Brothers Ltd., Sheffield
　　　John R. Fielder & Son Ltd., Titchfield
1962: Norman & Pring Ltd., Exeter
　　　Starkey Knight & Ford Ltd., Bridgwater
　　　Flowers Breweries Ltd., Luton which included
　　　　　J.W. Green and Flower & Sons Ltd.
1963: J. Nimmo & Son Ltd., Castle Eden
　　　West Country Brewery Holdings Ltd., Cheltenham
　　　　　(Cheltenham & Hereford Breweries Ltd.,
　　　　　Stroud Brewery Co. Ltd., and
　　　　　Spreckley Brothers Ltd.)
1964: Dutton's Blackburn Brewery Ltd., Blackburn
1965: E. Lacon & Co. Ltd., Great Yarmouth
1966: James Thompson & Co. Ltd., Barrow-in-Furness
　　　Rhymney Breweries Ltd., Rhymney

1967: Isaac Tucker & Co. Ltd., Gateshead
　　　Archibald Campbell, Hope & King Ltd.,
　　　　　Edinburgh
　　　Threlfalls Chesters Ltd., Liverpool
　　　Evan Evans, Bevan Ltd., Neath
　　　Fremlins Ltd., Maidstone
1968: Bentley's Yorkshire Breweries Ltd., Woodlesford
　　　Richard Whitaker & Sons Ltd., Halifax
　　　John Young & Co. Ltd., Musselburgh
　　　Cobb & Co. Ltd., Margate
　　　Combined Breweries (Holdings) Ltd., Ramsgate
　　　　　(Tomson & Wotton Ltd. and
　　　　　Gardner & Co. Ltd.)
　　　Strong & Co. of Romsey Ltd., Romsey
1971: Brickwoods Ltd., Portsmouth

approached by some of the smaller brewers asking for some form of help.

This was the start of what became known as the Whitbread Umbrella Scheme whereby Whitbread made informal trading agreements with a number of smaller brewery companies, enabling them to gain a certain amount of protection by means of the association, as well as opening up further markets for Whitbread products.

Because of this scheme certain of the associated companies benefitted by being able to make their own purchases of other breweries, so the association grew ever stronger. Cheltenham & Hereford, Strongs, Ruddles, Norman & Pring, Tennants, Marston, Thompson & Evershed, and Duttons were included in these early associations.

By the 1960s it was becoming obvious that these loose trading agreements were not enough, and several companies approached Whitbread with plans for even closer ties. From 1961 a series of take-overs took place which are listed in the panel on the previous page.

It must be remembered that many of those listed were old established brewers with long histories of their own, and some had earlier absorbed other brewers, so that a grand total of some 400 names can be listed.

As the mergers progressed it became evident that there was much duplication with regard to depots and vehicles, so a period of rationalisation began, at the end of which in 1971 no fewer than 15 breweries, 24 bottling stores and 54 depots had been closed. Parallel to this was a simplification of the transport fleet, with many of the 'non-standard' vehicles being replaced by vehicles which best suited the trade, with others being merely sold off as surplus to requirements.

At this time Whitbread could fairly be described as a Nationwide brewer and was rated as number three in the league table of British brewing companies.

Whilst all this was going on it was decided to give the company a new image, and a darker brown was adopted for the fleet colour and the old hinds head insignia replaced by a new design of Tankard, with the name and trademark being put on a red panel. Later, in 1982 another change was made and a redesigned hinds head with Est. 1742 adopted for signing vehicles as well as all the other company publicity.

Above: During the period of the 'Umbrella' scheme which established a trading agreement between Whitbread and a handful of other brewing companies in the 1950s, a few vehicles were sold to companies within the scheme. One of them was this 1948 Dennis 'Max' which was originally part of the Chiswell Street delivery fleet. Now with a replacement body and painted in City Brewery colours it stands partly loaded in the brewery yard at Exeter of Norman & Pring Ltd in 1957. For a 1950s vehicle the Dennis 'Max' embodied features that would not be out of place forty years later, such as the Dennis oil engine with its high camshafts, short pushrods and four-valves-per-cylinder, plus a five-speed gearbox which incorporated a top-speed overdrive operated by a pre-selector mechanism.

Left: One of the special vehicles in the Whitbread fleet was the Seddon articulated outfit S97 with its two semi-trailers: a four-stall horsebox and a semi-lowloader. Purchased for the transport of the famous Whitbread Shire Horses, the Carrimore low-loading horsebox was of the four-stall loose-box type with a section for the grooms, feed and tackle at the front end. By means of the patented Carrimore coupling there was a very small gap between tractor and trailer, and the Seddon tractor was a 5S9/2 model with low ratio rear axle. The horsebox had two loading ramps on the offside and carried display panels advertising the destination of the horses as well as individual name-boards including an ID-type photograph of each horse carried! During the summer months the tractor was kept busy shuttling between London and the north of England usually, first with the drays and then delivering the horses to hired stabling. In collaboration with the local Whitbread depot, the horse teams would carry out deliveries to local outlets with the drays suitably emblazoned with Mackeson advertising boards. The holiday areas of the Fylde coast were a particular target for the Sales Drives, and every opportunity was taken to gain maximum publicity because of the high profile achieved by the famous Whitbread Shires.

Left: With much emphasis being placed on the expansion of Mackeson sales in off-licence premises and other brewers houses, a number of Austin GV3 model vans were put into service during the 1950s in order to dispense point-of-sale material. These vans were rated at 10cwt capacity and were very attractive with the black and silver livery adopted for the Mackeson brand stout, as well as being liked by the display drivers because of their comfort and brisk performance, for they were based on the current version of the Austin 'Hampshire' saloon.

Top right: The Advertising Department were responsible for what became known as the 'Display Van', it being purely a promotional vehicle carrying only advertising material. Seen here in Mackeson's guise, the name-boards and display panels could be changed to promote any other products if desired, but it carried the Mackeson message for much of its life. This was the period when, like many other brewing companies, Whitbread was trying to get some of its products available in areas where the company had few if any outlets. The van was based on the Austin 'Three-Way' 25-cwt van chassis and carried equipment to provide illumination for the side panels and roof lights. It spent much of its time in company with the horse teams on sales drives in the north of England.

Left: Although some of the rigid 80-barrel tankers were equipped to tow trailers, the number of trailer tanks was few, so for orders of 120 barrels two vehicles had to be used, such as on this occasion in July 1957, when considerable quantities of Mackeson stout were required in the Devon area to quench the thirst of summer holiday-makers. The scene is the cattle market close to Norman & Pring's brewery in Exeter with At126 and S107, Atkinson 80-barrel and Seddon 40-barrel tanks respectively, patiently awaiting their drivers for the journey back to London. Note that both vehicles have Mackeson advertising headboards fitted above the normal Whitbread illuminated sign-boards as part of the continuing sales drive for the stout, and that conversely the radiator badges have been removed from the vehicles in an effort to reduce the advertising of the vehicle manufacturers!

Above: Following upon the success of Flowers with their Keg Bitter, several other brewers followed suit with their own types of pressurised draught beers of which Whitbread was one, marketing the famous Tankard. This style of beer dispensing, using pressurised metal containers together with the necessary carbon dioxide cylinders, beer coolers and all the ancillary piping and controls, was completely foreign to most public house tenants and managers, so some training was necessary. The importance of correct installation, operation and cleaning of the dispensing system, was met by the creation of special departments or at least expanded cellar management teams, and a small fleet of light vans was maintained in order to service the equipment and attend to any calls for help from the houses concerned. Early vans used were the Austin HV6 model of the current A55 car-derived range, and they were smartly turned out in a medium blue with a darker blue panel complete with the House of Whitbread logo of the period.

Left: J.W. Green of Luton introduced some striking new vehicles to the brewery world in the late 1940s with their fleet of Commer articulated streamlined vans, which incorporated sliding roofs for overhead loading. These were followed in the late 1950s by a wholly new fleet of maximum capacity artics using Atkinson T746 tractor units coupled to the recently introduced York Freightmaster van semi-trailers. These had been bought in order to serve the outlying locations at Grantham, Tunbridge Wells, Sunderland, Ashwell and Royston and their giant sides were put to use advertising the famous Brewmaster, plus the recently introduced Flowers Keg Bitter which was the precursor of the pressurised keg beers so widely used today.

Above right & middle: The six-wheel Dennis Pax Vs. were the first 'standardised' local delivery vehicles which were obtained in great numbers and turned out in a variety of brewery colours. Dennis Brothers themselves used several different brewery paint schemes in their advertisements such as Starkey, Knight & Ford and Norman & Pring. Here we picture another couple of them — Flowers and Duttons.

Bottom right: Finished in the nationwide livery used on the fleet during the 1970s, is this Ford D-series tractor and Hands step-frame semi-trailer with chain and post sides, which came from the Bentley's Yorkshire Breweries fleet. Although finished in Whitbread brown the tractor still carries its original fleet number 14.

Left: With the advent of relaxed legislation in 1964 which allowed for vehicles to gross up to a maximum of 32 tons on five axles, the company tackled the situation in two ways. The new regulations made it possible to increase the largest tank capacity from 80 barrels to 120 barrels, but tri-axle running gear was necessary if a two-axle tractor was used. For cask, keg, bottled and canned beer loads longer flat trailers were acquired and these were mounted on tandem running gear making the use of a three-axle tractor unit necessary to achieve maximum capacity. The six axle outfit shown here was still illegal in those days, and was merely used for shunting purposes within the confines of Oakley Road Brewery, Luton.

BRAND NEWS

So far as we have been able to discover Whitbread's colour scheme for its vehicles at least, was originally green with white lettering. In 1925 the change was made to brown with gold colour lettering and lining, and it remained that way with only minor modifications until the darker brown livery with a red panel came into use in 1967.

During the period 1922 to 1936 the Bottling Stores fleet was allowed to display the Prince of Wales feathers insignia on their vehicles, but somewhat surprisingly one of the company directors took exception to this and remarked that it was "a concession to the modern craze for propaganda and display".

With much money being spent on advertising Mackeson Stout in the post-war years, a decision was made to paint certain vehicles in that livery of silver and black, with the label design being put on the cab doors. Originally this was applied to some of the tankers operating from Chiswell Street, but later it was extended to other delivery vehicles as well as some light vans used by the Advertising department.

In the mid 1950s an Austin 25cwt van had been acquired purely for the purpose of advertising some of the company's products, and this was painted a plain beige colour with removable panels for advertising Mackeson, Pale Ale or Final Selection according to requirements.

One small variation came with the advent of Whitbread Tankard in 1957 when a fleet of light vans for servicing the dispensing equipment was liveried in a pale blue adopted as the Tankard Bitter livery.

Even when the company started to expand in earnest during the 1960s, there was no move to capitalise on the increasing stock of beer brands, and turn the vehicles out in anything but the regular brown.

It was not until the 1980s that a decision was made to paint vehicles in an all-over brand image for particular beers, and this policy has now spread throughout the country for customer delivery vehicles, as well as being extended to bulk tankers and the primary fleet of long distance vehicles.

In the past few years some of the brandings have been varied and others replaced, according to the wishes of the advertising strategy decided upon. It is now possible to see vehicles turned out in the liveries of:

- Whitbread White Label • Whitbread Trophy •
- Whitbread Best Bitter • Fremlins Bitter •
- Flowers Fine Ales • Heineken Lager Beer •
- Stella Artois • Welsh Bitter •
- Boddington's Bitter • Best Scotch •
- Murphys Irish Stout • Castle Eden Ale •

Left: In 1920 the company acquired F.S. Stowell Ltd. of Ealing, a small company with just six off-licences, but it was not until the 1950s that the company made any attempt to expand its activities in the wine and spirit business. By the acquisition of several similar businesses during the 1960s the Stowell business expanded and in 1968 the title Stowells of Chelsea was adopted, with the headquarters being located in Britten Street, Chelsea which had served as a Whitbread depot on the site of an old brewery acquired in 1899. A livery of dark blue was later replaced by the two-tone blue as shown on this 19.. BMC FH model van, which had roller shutters on both sides as well as at the rear.

Above: Although not very bright, this early colour photograph shows a Bedford 0-type in the livery used on the Luton-based fleet of Flowers Breweries just after the takeover by J.W. Green, hence the two-tone green. Soon after a change was made to the all-over primrose yellow which had been a feature of the Flower & Sons of Stratford-upon-Avon fleet.

Right: This most unusual view is taken from the front cover of the October 1935 issue of the Bedford Transport Magazine, which as the name implies, was issued to operators and customers using Bedford commercial vehicles. The issue included several photographs of Bedfords in service with companies in the brewery trade, and three pages were devoted to a story of J.W. Green Ltd. and their Park Street West brewery at Luton — which was also the home town of Bedford trucks.

Below: A brilliant day in 'Pompey' highlights the sunburst trademark carried on the headboard of this batch of BMC Laird six-wheelers supplied to Brickwoods in 1970, just prior to the Whitbread takeover of the company. During this period many brewers were trying out low-loaders based on the concept of using smaller diameter wheels and tyres in order to reduce height, but having to resort to six wheels so as not to reduce payload. One Midlands brewer even resorted to specifying four axles on a similar chassis in the battle to maintain payloads while keeping heights as low as possible.

Left: This 1955 Thornycroft model PF/NR6 was one of a batch of the make used by Flowers Breweries Ltd. for long distance work following the launch of the new company in 1954. Both tankers and platform body types were in operation, but not for local delivery work as this posed photograph outside the Gibraltar Castle would suggest! Later bulk vehicles acquired by Flowers used AEC chassis even before the takeover of Thornycroft by AEC in 1961, indicating that the Southall product was preferred to those from Basingstoke.

Top right: Following the acquisition of so many large brewery concerns, the company was divided by the creation of operating companies to cover certain areas of the country. This 1966 Dennis 'Pax V', which was typical of the customer delivery fleet of the period, is seen in the all-over brown livery with the red name panels, but with the local company name on the door, which in this case is Whitbread (East Pennines) Ltd. for the vehicle is pictured at the old Woodlesford premises of Bentley's Yorkshire Breweries.

Middle right: Probably photographed when the vehicle was nearing the end of its brewery life, this 1961 Morris 7-tonner shows the bright yellow livery adopted for the fleet operated by E. Lacon & Co. Ltd. of Great Yarmouth. The vehicle dates from the period when the British Motor Corporation was offering a range of vehicles which embraced types originally marketed by both Austin and Morris, and there was much evidence of models produced with a variety of Austin, Morris or BMC badging.

Below right: Trunk vehicle operation of the mid 1970s was marked by the introduction of a number of Foden S83 tractor units to the fleet. One of these was photographed when actually at work with a double headboard trailer, and used on the cover of the Foden News for 1976 as shown here.

Left: In the early 1970s considerable thought was given to the production of a combination vehicle which could carry out a large number of deliveries in an area remote from the distribution depot. This idea bore fruit in the production of a six-wheel vehicle with four-wheel drawbar trailer, the front axle of which was actually a two-wheel dolly which was attached to a semi-trailer. The concept became known as the CDCU — Customer Delivery Combination Unit, and was first tried out with a Bedford KM vehicle. This photograph shows the second generation of the idea when a special Scammell six-wheeler was obtained.

Left: Continuing the trend of finishing vehicles in brand liveries, this Bedford TK is turned out in a blue and red colour scheme and lettered for the Beefeater chain of restaurants. It has been specially modified for the handling of demountable tanks in order to serve the cellar tanks used in some of the larger houses. The 5-barrel tanks are carefully positioned by fork truck and then secured to avoid movement by the moveable clamps which pass through one of each of the individual tanks' mounting feet. With the side curtains drawn the vehicle retains the appearance of a normal customer delivery vehicle and presents a good advertising image for Beefeater restaurants.

Below: What must rank as one of the most outstanding vehicle liveries is surely the Whitbread Trophy design as shown here on one of the Ford Cargo 16-tonne gvw delivery vehicles. This vehicle dates from the late 1980s and features bodywork by Marshall of Cambridge, mounted on a Ford engined chassis with rear steel springs, and with drop-frame engineered by Chassis Developments.

Right: The 1970s saw the curtain-sided style of bodywork come into prominence in the Whitbread customer delivery fleet. This 1978 Ford D-series model D1411 was scheduled for a maximum life of ten years, but during the 1980s, at a time when the larger pallet was introduced, a decision was taken to thoroughly overhaul a large section of the fleet in preference to following the normal replacement programme. This was necessary because of the extreme cost of replacing a large part of the fleet all in one year. This was also the period when the overall brown Whitbread livery was discontinued and individual brand names began to grace the fleet, bringing with them a new, fresh image.

Below: Seemingly dwarfed by the storage tanks at Exchange Brewery, this Ford Cargo curtain sided vehicle with matching close-coupled drawbar trailer marks a variation in the normal delivery pattern of the company. The vehicle operates on a schedule between Tinsley near Sheffield and the delivery area around Grimsby and Hull. What is not immediately obvious is that the outfit consists of demountable body units on both vehicle and trailer *(right)*, and the schedule calls for the body units to be demounted in the delivery area, and the empties picked up for the return journey to Tinsley. A similar operation is carried out from Shadsworth near Blackburn where a Scania and trailer outfit performs a comparable function serving an area around the Lake District.

As mentioned earlier, haulage contractors have played a significant part in the development of the Whitbread delivery service, and the arrangement continues subject to modifications to accommodate variations in demand.

During the 1970s a decision was made to contract out the delivery service for the take-home trade which consisted of one-trip packages. In 1982 this was extended significantly when a joint venture was instituted between the company and the National Freight Corporation by the setting up of Bar Delivery Services. This innovative arrangement established a full distribution service for the whole of metropolitan London and the northern Home Counties through a fleet of vehicles based at Kentish Town and Dunstable. The fleet included some of the earlier Whitbread Bedford TK twin-steer curtain sided type as shown here *(top left)*.

In 1989, with the acquisition of Boddingtons at Manchester, another contract was taken over, this time with TNT Contract Distribution operating a fleet of urban artics from a dedicated base at Wigan. A fleet of 25 Leyland 'Freighter' tractor units is employed, working with 13: 30ft and 20: 26ft 12-ton capacity single axle semi-trailers *(middle left)*.

Much of the present day contract hire fleet consists of the popular model FL617 Volvo with standard height chassis and bodywork adequate for the delivery of non-returnable packages to supermarkets and similar outlets. This particular vehicle *(below)* is finished in the attractive livery adopted for Murphy's Irish Stout and is one of the vehicles supplied by Tibbett & Britten.

At present the three main contracts are allocated on the basis of TNT for the Boddington fleet, a contract with Tibbett & Britten to handle the 'take-home' trade, and the London & Home Counties delivery service which is executed by Exel Logistics, successors to Bar Delivery Services.

Above: Into the last decade of the century the customer delivery fleet is predominantly Iveco-Ford and Volvo in the 16-17-tonne gross weight category. This normal height FL617 Volvo finished in the stunning livery of Stella Artois serves to show how a simple design can achieve a high visual impact. The vehicle is one of the contract fleet supplied by Tibbett & Britten.

Below: Resplendent in its all-white livery, this FL617 model Volvo represents the state of customer delivery mainstream development at the end of the 1980s. With a drop frame engineered by Volvo at Irvine, resulting in a 24" deck height and incorporating their rear air suspension specifically modified to suit. The curtain-sided bodywork is by Marshall of Cambridge.

Left: Pictured at rest after an exhausting test period, the Ford Cargo 3828 and Foden 4300-series tractors pose with the Crane Fruehauf curtain-sider semi-trailer during the MIRA stability tests. Note the large under-chassis anti-roll device necessary to prevent the vehicle overturning during tests which caused the trailer wheels to actually lift off the ground on occasions as the outfit was pushed to the limit in high speed cornering.

Top right: The design of maximum capacity vehicle for the primary fleet of the company has received its fair share of attention from transport engineers, resulting in this Mercedes-Benz articulated outfit with curtain sider bodywork. The tractor is the 1733 model, the designation indicating a 17-tonne gross weight tractor with 330bhp engine. Other designations displayed on the radiator grille indicate that it is a second generation in the makers Powerliner series, it has the ABS controlled system of braking, the driver has the advantage of EPS power-assisted gear changing and the type was voted Truck of the Year in 1990.

Middle left: A further development of the lightweight trend in customer delivery vehicles came in 1991 with the introduction of an experimental six-wheel version of the MAN middleweight. This vehicle, shown here in the striking black and yellow adopted for the Boddingtons fleet livery, has similar advantages of the four wheel version but offers an additional payload capacity of 2.7-tonnes, and provide for a deck height of 28"

Bottom right: For the 1990s the Primary Fleet which is engaged in the long distance distribution of both bulk tank and packaged products from the main centres of production will consist of Mercedes-Benz tractors and tri axle trailers with either curtain-sided or tank bodywork. At present all of this Primary Fleet is turned out in Heineken green, but this will soon change so that the tractor units will be finished in a completely different colour. This will enable units to be switched to operate with different liveried trailers, without the harsh clash of colours which might otherwise occur

Left: Another eye-catching livery is that adopted for Strong Country Bitter, shown here on a 1987 Ford suitably posed outside the Dog & Crook. This 1615-model Cargo is typical of the low-loader design of the period with front-mounted steel exhaust, steel springs front and rear, curtain-sider style body and most importantly a low floor height.

The company is justly proud of its long transport history, and has striven to maintain a road vehicle fleet which reflects its concern with quality of product, as well as service to the customer. In recent years the cost of transport generally has come under close scrutiny with a view to providing a high standard of service at a reasonable cost, achieving high productivity whilst maintaining safety. One aspect of staying ahead is being able to visualise future trends, and in this respect three prototype concept vehicles are just entering service in order to study their feasibility under operating conditions.

These three innovative designs go to prove that as our story closes on the first 250 years of its transport history, the company remains in the forefront of distribution technology, and can face the challenges of 2000 and beyond with confidence.

The first *(top)* is a further progression of the proven curtain-sided type of body by Don-Bur, but this time with a short, centre-bogie trailer added to the MAN six-wheel design mentioned earlier.

Second *(middle right)* is an Iveco-Ford 'New Cargo' six-wheeler with a Marshall Combi-Roll type of curtain-side body, with the curtain being rolled up vertically but with the aid of a centre furling bar to provide some stiffening.

Last of the trio *(bottom right)* is another 'New Cargo' six-wheel chassis this time fitted with a gull-wing style body by Mostard of Holland. In this design it is possible to gain clear access to the load in a matter of seconds by means of the solid side panels which are swung outward and upwards easily by one person. The side panel is hinged horizontally and when folded in half is held up above the roof line whilst the delivery is made.